IN MY FATHER'S FOOTSTEPS

My Journey into Lakota Country

WILLLIAM MATSON

Reel Contact Publishing
Spearfish, SD

In My Father's Footsteps—My Journey into Lakota Country
by William Matson

Published 2020 by Reel Contact Publishing
www.reelcontact.com
Spearfish, SD 57783
info@reelcontact.com

Paperback ISBN: 978-1-7358670-0-7

Ebook ISBN: 978-1-7358670-1-4

Dedicated to:

Mae Matson
Emerson and JoAnne Matson
Robert Matson and Mariellen Matson Tayler
All Our Benefactors Who Made This Book Possible

Contents

Foreword

IN 2016, I WROTE the book, *Crazy Horse: The Lakota Warrior's Life and Legacy*, based on the Crazy Horse family's oral history, as told to me by family members of Crazy Horse: Edward Clown, Floyd Clown Sr., Doug War Eagle, and Don Red Thunder. During the early portion of the book-signing tour, I knew there would be questions about my relationship to the family, but I underestimated just how many.

As of the writing of this current book, we have held 317 book signings for the first book. Our audiences invariably asked "How did you meet?" and "Why did they pick you?" But both the family and I believe what they were really asking is: "What is a white guy from the West Coast doing with this sacred Native family? Why would this family, of all families, trust a member of the race of people that had disenfranchised them from their land and way of life? Why did he get to hear their most treasured stories?"

Good questions.

With this book, I incorporate the answers to those questions, trying to put them to rest for those who could not attend our signings.

The first few chapters give a background of who I was prior to meeting the Crazy Horse grandsons, and why I needed to meet them. The next few chapters tell how I earned enough of their trust for them to tell me their story. The final chapters recount our journey together, along with my meeting and working with Sitting Bull's great grandson, Ernie LaPointe. The entire book details my search for the truth. It's really an incredible adventure.

Chapter One

Vietnam

IN THE SUMMER OF 1966, I was awkward. Immature. I felt inadequate. I had just graduated from high school. Now I was supposedly a grownup.

I spent the first two years as a "grownup" at the University of Washington. I hadn't partied in high school. My mother had watched me like a hawk to insure I didn't. So after I got to college, I felt the need to know what partying was all about. I partied nearly every night—and I promptly flunked out of college.

The Vietnam War was being waged. The US government was drafting young men into the armed services like there was no tomorrow. It wasn't long before I got the "Greetings" letter from Uncle Sam, telling me they had drafted me into the army. I didn't want to go. But I had to.

I did the only thing any reasonable person would do. I made a vow to dedicate myself towards surviving my mandatory two years of military service.

In retrospect, it was my army experience that transformed me from a boy into a man. It was there I gained the confidence to make "impossible" things possible.

But to understand how my thinking developed, long before I met the Crazy Horse family, to understand what events I experienced that enabled me to let my heart lead me, and ultimately to receive the honor to hear and then tell their family's oral history—we need to go back to a place called Vietnam, on April 30, 1969.

When I first stepped off the plane in Vietnam, the hot, humid air felt heavy in my lungs. My body felt like a licked postage stamp. The humidity sapped my energy as I walked down the steps from a United Airlines passenger plane onto the tarmac.

I was nervous and scared.

My first night there I slept on a cot inside a great big tent with the rest of the newly arrived. Rats as big as full-grown cats were everywhere. All night long they scurried along the tent supports above me. I laid awake that first night fearing one would fall and land on me.

The next morning those in charge of our in-country processing sent us to a two-day orientation class. I remember little from that class. One thing I do remember was them requiring us to brush our teeth with a grainy, awful-tasting toothpaste. They warned us not to swallow or get it onto our clothing because it would make us sick or permanently stain our uniform. Its purpose was to keep our teeth healthy for an entire year. What it did to the rest of our bodies was anybody's guess. But in the army's defense, brushing was not an option in the remote fields of Vietnam.

They then whisked me and seven other newly arrived medics away to a resupply convoy. I found myself a passenger in a deuce-and-a-half (two-and-one-half ton) truck cab on its way to the Americal Division in Chu Lai.

From Chu Lai they sent me to a medical unit in the 196th Light Infantry Brigade at a place called LZ Baldy. Our unit later moved north to LZ Hawk Hill. (LZ stood for landing zone, which is like a fort. Strands of razor-sharp, coiled barbwire surrounded the LZ. Bunkers populated the perimeter every hundred yards. Soldiers manned the bunkers twenty-four hours a day.)

During my initial two months, I assisted at the medic station. I gave shots, filled sandbags, and did my best to make myself indispensable to keep from being sent to a combat unit. They finally assigned me as a temporary platoon medic for Bravo Company, 2nd of the 1st Infantry Battalion, on July 6, 1969.

William in Vietnam 1969

There I substituted for their regular medic, Doc Elliott. They had sent Elliott back to the LZ so they could treat him for jungle rot, which is a tropical infection that eats skin and muscle. If left untreated, it can result in amputation. Spending days walking through the wet Vietnamese rice paddies while on patrol was the primary cause of the infection.

I had been with Bravo Company only four days when I experienced my first fire fight (battle), on July 10. With my platoon mates' help, I patched up our wounded platoon leader from the middle of a hotly contested rice paddy. I must confess I wasn't overly enthusiastic about responding when I first heard them call "Medic." I really didn't know what I was doing when I finally made it to his side. But I didn't want to be the reason he died.

One guy in our platoon was a cocky New Yorker named Fox. Everyone called him Foxy. I never learned his first name. Full names were not something I learned during my tour, at least not while I was with a "grunt" (infantry) unit operating in a hostile area. My reasoning was if I got too close to someone and lost them in battle, I might not handle it well. I have never been good at accepting death and I knew not everyone would make it home.

Foxy's peers regarded him as a man of great instincts— instincts that kept them alive. He was one of three soldiers that led me to our platoon leader, a second lieutenant, shot twice in the upper thigh. He had lost an inordinate amount of blood.

While at the lieutenant's side, I saw the fear in his eyes. A fear greater than my own. Somehow that gave me strength.

"Am I going to live?" he asked in a shaky voice.

I didn't know the answer, but I told him "yes." I didn't want him to give up.

I put a bandage on his wound. It was all I had. Then a Medevac (a helicopter that transported wounded to a hospital), picked him up and took him away. Thankfully, he lived.

After we returned to the LZ, my platoon buddies expressed their appreciation for my efforts. In my mind, I didn't think I had done anything noteworthy. Putting on a bandage and telling him he would be okay? Anybody could have done that. Their gratitude made me feel awkward. They were the ones that escorted me to his side. They were the ones who kept me safe with their covering fire. They were the genuine heroes. Not me. I'm not sure I would have even found our platoon leader among the thigh-high, slender rice leaves without their help.

Two days later, in the early morning of July 12, we did a road sweep outside our LZ, sweeping the road with metal detectors in search of enemy land mines. After we finished our sweep, Foxy encouraged me to stay and spend time with him and the Vietnamese soda girls. I wanted to learn as many survival skills as I could. I instinctively knew if I stayed close to Foxy, I could survive this war. Two of our other platoon members also stayed out with us.

Soda girls were teenagers or youthful adult women who followed the GIs around on bicycles. They sold warm beer and soda for one Military Pay Certificate, known as MPC. An MPC dollar was equivalent to a US dollar. The soda girls would not accept their own country's currency, the Vietnamese piastre, because it was too volatile. So each soda girl picked one GI to give free drinks to, but only if that GI agreed to be her "boyfriend." If he agreed, she gave him a bead necklace to wear to show he was spoken for. She did this because occasionally the military changed the color and design of the MPC. A new design made any previously issued MPC obsolete. Only authorized military personnel could exchange the obsolete for the new. That's why a boyfriend was important. Someone she could reliably ask to exchange her old money for the new.

A cute teenage soda girl asked me to be her boyfriend. I agreed. As a result, she gave me a bright orange and green pop bead necklace. I had hoped for something more subtle, but the pop beads were what I got, so I wore them. She also gave me a warm can of Budweiser.

Spotting my newly acquired beer, Foxy showed me how to make it cold. He bought a block of ice from our "girlfriends" and rolled my beer rapidly on it. Then handed it to me. I popped it open with a "church key" (can opener), waited for it to finish spraying its built-up energy, and then drank it. It was cold. I was impressed.

For the next hour we sat and drank our ice-cooled beers while flirting with the soda girls. As I sipped my beer, I wondered what would happen if the enemy attacked us just then. We only numbered four. So I asked Foxy if he had any concerns.

He laughed. "Don't worry. You're covered. The soda girls are here. If there was any danger, they would have *di di mau*-ed a long time ago, Doc."

They nicknamed all medics "Doc." *Di di mau* is Vietnamese for hurry or run away.

Foxy and I had a blast talking about the lives we had lived back in the "world" (a GI expression for the United States), and we quickly formed a bond.

As morning faded into afternoon, we headed back to the LZ. Foxy and I walked together down the same road we had earlier swept for mines. Our other two platoon brothers trailed us by about fifteen meters. One brother went by the name of Richard Fell. I remember his full name for a reason. As we continued to saunter back to the LZ, I suddenly heard a grating noise that sounded like wheels skidding on the dirt road behind me. When I turned around, I saw Fell, hurled into the air like a rag doll, falling belly up onto the road.

A speeding American jeep had gone out of control and hit him.

I rushed to his aid. Upon kneeling by his side, I found his eyes open, covered in dust and lifeless. He was pale and had no pulse.

He was not breathing.

His tongue had slid into the back of his throat.

All around me the soda girls were crying and screaming "he's dead." Foxy and my other platoon buddy were vehemently cussing out the jeep driver for hitting Fell. Ashamed, the driver shrank back into his seat and radioed the LZ for help. I somehow entered a world where everything became surreal. The cries, screams, and cussing receded into the distant background.

I stuck my finger in his mouth to dislodge his tongue, which was blocking his airway, but to no avail. His tongue was too slippery.

Then I remembered a film on tracheotomies I had seen during my medical training. I thought if I could open his windpipe using this method, I could get him breathing again. I took out my bayonet and pushed the point against his windpipe. My bayonet was dull. I failed to penetrate his windpipe as I pushed harder and harder on his throat. Suddenly I became frightened that once my bayonet broke through his skin, it might pierce his neck all the way to the ground. I know that sounds silly, but extreme situations make you think extreme thoughts.

I put my bayonet down.

Then I remembered I had a hollow plastic tube in the top left breast pocket of my uniform. I had picked it up at the medic station for no reason. It had seemed to call to me from a forgotten corner of the station. So, I pulled it out of my pocket and shoved it down his throat. Thankfully, it opened his windpipe. I began giving him mouth to mouth through the plastic tube while the sole passenger from the jeep pounded on his chest to get his heart beating again. We did this for about ten minutes. Those ten minutes felt like an eternity.

Finally, an ambulance dispatched from the LZ rolled up, carrying our battalion surgeon, Doctor Wong. He was a South Korean national who had joined the US Army hoping to become a US citizen. He had expected to work in a hospital. But he was as close to the front lines as a doctor ever gets. And now, being outside the safe confines of the LZ, he was even further outside his comfort zone.

After glancing around nervously for any hidden enemy combatants, he knelt down and quickly examined Fell. Then he stood up. He slowly shook his head, looked me in the eye and said, "I'm sorry Matson, but he's dead."

I didn't believe him.

If Fell was going to die, he would have told me—as non-sensible as that sounds, that's what I believed. I was still that young.

We then loaded Fell onto a stretcher and placed him in the ambulance.

The ambulance sped off towards our field hospital inside the LZ. I rode in the back with Fell and continued to give him mouth to mouth. Doctor Wong sat in the front, encouraging the driver to hurry back to the LZ. Foxy and my other platoon buddy followed us in the jeep that had hit him. The jeep had remained undamaged because of its thick armor.

When we got to the hospital, we carried Fell in on the stretcher. We set him down on an operating table. Doctor Wong's medical assistant inserted an I-V into his arm.

And then something remarkable happened.

Fell sat up and asked what had happened.

There is no way I can describe what I felt. My heart jumped through my throat. It was the best feeling I ever experienced in my life.

William with a Vietnamese Army scout, 1970

After Fell settled back down on his stretcher, I felt Foxy's arm draping over my shoulder. He whispered, "That was something, Doc."

I didn't know how to reply. I was shaking. I said nothing. My efforts had been an act of desperation. I had not revived him through some special skill. I had revived him because something inside me told me he was supposed to live.

On the way back to our platoon, Foxy walked by my side while I tried to process what had just happened. Unexpectedly, the head of my medical unit, First Lieutenant Simonetti, intercepted us. After congratulating me on saving Fell, he gave me an order, "Matson, Elliott's jungle rot has cleared up. He'll be rejoining Bravo. Your job is done here. This afternoon there's a chopper leaving for Charlie Company. That will be your new unit. You need to be on the chopper pad at fourteen-hundred hours. You'll be joining them in the field."

Sadness replaced my euphoria. I had grown to love Bravo Company. I really didn't want to leave them.

As soon as Simonetti left, Foxy spun me around and said, "You ain't going. You're staying with us."

In the brief time I had been with Bravo, I had developed a powerful connection with the guys. Especially Foxy. "I want to stay, but I have to go. I'll get in trouble," I replied. Disobeying an order, especially while in a war zone, was high risk. It could land me in a military prison.

"Doc, I'm going to tell all the guys and we'll make sure you ain't going nowhere. You're part of us now."

Foxy was just a private. I did not understand how he expected to buck the brass and keep me in Bravo

Company. But true to his word, he told the rest of the platoon. They watched over me like a bunch of mother hens to make sure I did not wander away or end up being escorted to Charlie Company without their knowledge.

Then fourteen hundred hours arrived.

I was eager not to cause trouble. I said, "I got to go. I don't want to, but I got to."

"We're coming with you," Foxy stated matter-of-factly.

So with my rucksack in hand, I headed to the chopper pad with the entire platoon following me. Lt. Simonetti was waiting. The platoon stopped directly behind me.

The lieutenant paused and surveyed the scene.

"Say your goodbyes, the chopper will be here any minute."

Then their reasons for accompanying me became clear. From behind me I heard Foxy shout, "He ain't going."

The lieutenant paused again. His eyes found Foxy, "This is a matter between Matson and me."

"He ain't going," Foxy shouted again.

Lt. Simonetti was not about to back down. Not to a lowly private. "Matson, put on your rucksack and come with me," he ordered.

Foxy didn't speak this time. Instead, he chambered a shell in his M-16 rifle. The rest of the platoon followed suit. They locked and loaded on the lieutenant, who froze. It had escalated into something that I would never have imagined.

I just stood there between the lieutenant and my platoon mates, holding my breath. Afraid to move. I could feel and hear my blood pulsating.

With locked and loaded rifles pointed in his direction, the lieutenant's self-assurance evaporated like a drop of water on a red-hot skillet. He gulped air and sputtered, "But maybe we can work something out so that Matson can stay with your unit."

Several voices behind me grunted "Yeah" and "You do that."

"I'll make sure it happens," Simonetti said meekly.

Foxy and the rest of Bravo lowered their weapons, and the lieutenant slinked away.

My body melted in relief. I did not know if my new platoon brothers would have shot the lieutenant that day. I was just thankful that I never had to find out.

All my platoon mates shook my hand to congratulate me on staying. I was happy and numb at the same time. Happy I could stay. Numb over what had just happened. Like myself, they all just wanted to survive this war. Bringing one of their own back to life made them think I was more skilled than the other medics. I was not. But their reaction motivated me to try to live up to their expectations, anyway.

In listening to my gut, I had saved a life. I was further rewarded by being able to serve in the platoon I most desired. The army gave me an Army Commendation Medal for saving Fell's life. To me, all of this was a potent argument for trusting my gut. It had been my gut that had told me to ignore the doctor's expertise and keep trying to save Fell's life. The concept of being an "expert" lost its validity. It is something that became a big factor in my pursuit of the Crazy Horse family's story even after reading numerous books and research on Crazy Horse by so-called "experts."

A month later the brass pulled me from the field. My father had written a letter to our Congressman complaining that my eyesight was not adequate enough to keep me safe in the field. As a result, the Congressman had ordered a Congressional investigation into my ability to see properly. Thus, the brass brought me in to cover their asses.

After a subsequent eye examination, they deemed me unfit for combat. At first I was thrilled, but soon I became bored having to stay in the rear area. I missed the camaraderie and adrenaline rushes I had experienced in the field. So, I asked if I could return to the field. The brass told me I would have to sign a waiver. I did.

I never told my parents about the waiver. I just told them I got fit for a proper pair of glasses and thanked them.

Unfortunately, I was not reassigned to Bravo but to Alpha Company instead. I was with Alpha until just before Thanksgiving when I was wounded with shrapnel from a 60mm mortar round while out on patrol.

I took three pieces of shrapnel in my left leg and one in the left temple of my head.

Once I healed, they sent me back to the field with Charley Company, after two of their medics were killed after sitting on a booby trap. I was the only medic available at the time.

After my tour ended and it was time to go home, only three of the original seven medics that I had entered Vietnam with would fly home with me. They had killed four of us. Two of our four survivors had suffered combat wounds. I counted myself just plain lucky to be one of the wounded.

When I returned to the "world," the army scheduled an appointment for me to have my wounds looked at by some "experts" to determine disability compensation. I

William with a buddy, Rudy, on last day in Vietnam

didn't show up. I had had enough of the military. Their rules. Their regulations. Their "experts."

As I entered civilian life, I found my time in Vietnam had given me a lack of tolerance for everyday life. I could not understand why people got excited over saving a nickel on a grocery item. Going from saving lives to saving nickels was difficult.

I missed the adrenaline rushes. So I replaced my adrenaline highs with marijuana highs. Every morning I got up and smoked a bowl of marijuana, ate, smoked another bowl, and went back to bed. I repeated this every day for about a year. I was a mess until a pretty redhead came into my life. She gave me a fresh kind of adrenaline rush—love.

She convinced me to give up smoking marijuana and lead a sober, drug-free life. She took over my heart. I went cold turkey and stopped.

Her name was Sandy Plumb. We married on November 22, 1971. I embraced the role as her provider and by my thirtieth birthday, together we owned a beautiful, two-story home on six acres with an in-ground swimming pool, a large barn with a hayloft, six large horse stalls and tack room, eight thoroughbred racehorses, a creek with spawning salmon, and a beautiful view of the rural countryside. We also owned forty acres of farmland on the Twisp River in eastern Washington and five acres of vacant land inside the Olympia, Washington, city limits.

We were the envy of our friends. We were living the American dream.

Sandy kept me straight. Unfortunately, I felt my life was narrow and unfulfilling. Spending all my time concentrating on accumulating wealth was too confining. I felt like a robot. I no longer believed in what I was doing. I had to ask myself, "Is money and material things all there is to life?"

Sandy didn't understand my thinking. She wanted to continue to accumulate and build for our retirement. But for me, I reasoned, retirement just wasn't in my vocabulary. Life beckoned me to do something greater than just save for retirement. Thus, the glow in our relationship dimmed. Following the so-called American dream had not made me happy.

We separated in 1980 and divorced in 1982.

After the divorce, I re-arranged my priorities. I now had the freedom to pursue what I wanted. I let my heart run free to go after my original dream, the dream I grew up with as a child when I was alone in my bedroom daydreaming: about making a movie. One that would affect people's lives and make the world a better place. Once that dream re-ignited, my adrenaline came back like an old friend.

However, my decision came with fallout. My inability to afford the things I needed to survive replaced my inability to pursue the things I wanted to do. As a result, I lost my house for failure to maintain payments. I became a broken man, financially.

When I finally found alternative ways of surviving, I still put most everything I earned into trying to finance a movie.

This went on for years—until one fateful day. . . .

Chapter Two
Dad's Dying Wish

MY HEART WAS HEAVY as I walked down the hospital hallway. The smell of sickness permeated the air. Near the end of the hall, I found my father's room and entered.

He was painfully thin. An I-V bottle hung above his hospital bed, dripping rhythmically into a long, thin plastic tube leading to a needle embedded in his left forearm. A white bandage not wide enough to cover the bruises left from previous injections anchored it.

His body trembled in pain. The pain caused him to shut his eyes tightly as his gnarled hands grasped and clawed at his chest. I was sure he was unaware I had entered the room. My mother was sitting by his side.

"Hi, Dad."

An uncomfortable silence followed.

"He's having a rough time," my mother finally said, filling the silence for him.

I stood by his side, searching for a way to communicate.

Nine months earlier, Dad had called and told me, in a relaxed and measured way, he had been diagnosed with lymphoma, and that the doctors were optimistic they had caught it in time. The news stunned me, but his upbeat tone eased my fears. He had always been mentally strong, and his optimism was in keeping with his character. If anybody knew how to beat cancer, it was Dad. However, unknown to me, his words belied his genuine state.

I was living in Portland, Oregon, and in the middle of producing and directing my first feature film. I had stubbornly held on to my dream, and now it was finally coming true. Much of my adult life had been invested in raising the money to make a film. Every bone in my body hungered for it. To date, the amount of money I put together was insufficient by any reasonable standard, but I decided to make my film anyway. Probably not my smartest move—but I wasn't getting younger. I had just turned fifty.

William on the set of his film "Sex, Love, and Karaoke" 1997

My film was a musical, with singing and dancing. The problem was, most of the actors I cast couldn't really dance, even though they said they could. They made stiff, jerky motions that reminded me of malfunctioning marionettes. To make matters worse, some couldn't sing, either. My impatience to fulfill my dream had blinded me to the realities of making my motion picture professionally presentable enough to woo distributors. I now realized my chances of success were remote. But quitting was never in my DNA. Not knowing when to quit, however, can be a serious flaw.

I had to eat and live. For several months I lived off apples and single-serve Tillamook cheese snacks. I budgeted about two dollars per day for food. My bills were so far in arrears I had to close my bank accounts. Any money I put into them was garnished immediately.

I made agreements with people that required me to fulfill obligations, down the road. Advances from those agreements paid the expenses of making my movie. Uncertainty hovered over my ability to pay it all back. Living under this kind of pressure was a daily routine. I no longer was in charge of my dream—my dream was in charge of me. Some of my obligations were already coming due. I needed to take care of them or suffer losing all the progress I thought I had made.

Now my father needed me. However, he knew of my predicament and seemed to understand it better than I did. He said to spend all the time I needed to finish my film. By the end of his call, he assured me he would defeat the cancer. I believed him.

For nearly six months, we talked on the phone a few times each month, and he would tell me the chemotherapy was working. He said his chances of recovery were excellent—until suddenly they weren't.

He was now in Good Samaritan Hospital in Puyallup, Washington. I had no choice but to go see him. My conscience would not permit otherwise. I put my film on hold.

I found him lying in a hospital room shared with another man. He was in high spirits and pleased to see me.

Emerson Nels Matson, 1997

My father, Emerson Nels Matson, was born on May 23, 1926, in Seattle, Washington. He was the son of Anna Elizabeth David and Nels Isaac Matson. He was the first of three children and their only boy.

Emerson's father, Nels, was a jack of all trades and possessed a playful sense of humor. His mother, Anna, loved the outdoors, her family, cooking, and church. She would have fit well in a Norman Rockwell painting.

As a youngster, my father's dream was to be a professional baseball player. In 1938 he won the "Old Woodenface" pitching contest at Seattle's minor league baseball park, Sick's Seattle Stadium. "Old Woody," as they nicknamed it, was a contest to see which boy aged thirteen years old or younger could throw the most baseballs through a wooden window frame from sixty feet away. Those that went through were strikes. That day, Dad threw the most strikes. Instant fame resulted—his picture appeared in the local newspapers.

His success caused dreams of becoming a major-league baseball pitcher to feel real. However, his parents deemed this unrealistic, and they spent a great deal of time trying to steer him in different directions. They urged him to make a different career choice—a safe one. His grandmother Katie advised him that, since the family was related to Ralph Waldo Emerson, being a prominent writer was in his blood. The family encouraged him to go to college and learn a professional skill. Anything but baseball.

Old Woodenface Competition in Seattle, 1938

Emerson Matson accepts a watch for winning "Old Wooden Face" pitching contest, 1938

He must have listened well to their arguments, because they were the same arguments he would use on me for wanting to make movies—he and my mother felt being a lawyer would be the best vocation for me to pursue.

Nevertheless, the newspaper articles outweighed any vocational recommendations his parents could muster. Dad felt all he had to do was finish high school, try out for a major-league baseball team, and be discovered. He graduated in June 1944.

World War II was raging at the time, so the freedom to pursue a major-league baseball tryout disappeared. Graduating only alerted his local draft board of his availability. They drafted him into the US Army a few weeks after graduation and assigned him to a basic training unit run by the 7th Cavalry at Camp Stoneham in Pittsburg, California.

The 7th Cavalry had a prominent history. On June 25, 1876, Lieutenant Colonel George Armstrong Custer led the 7th Cavalry into battle against a Lakota and Cheyenne camp. The Battle of the Little Bighorn ensued. Custer and his men were wiped out. Most Americans remembered them as brave, patriotic martyrs.

My Dad's 7th Cavalry drill instructor attempted to capitalize on this flattering interpretation to help instill pride in his unit. Pride that their unit had always been victorious and always would be. He would ask his young recruits: "Who won the Battle of the Little Bighorn?" The expected answer, of course, was "Custer and the 7th Cavalry."

My Dad was taught to tell the truth. So he did. He told the drill sergeant the Indians had won. He knew the Lakota and Cheyenne were still standing at the end, not Custer and his men—so how could it be said Custer had won?

It made his drill instructor mad. He ridiculed my father, forced him to do extra physical training and perform unpleasant duties.

The injustice of his drill instructor's reaction made my dad angry—angry enough to hold a grudge for the rest of his life, angry enough to pass that grudge along to me. Here my journey to meet the Crazy Horse family and Sitting Bull's great grandchildren started, even though my heart would not start beating for another four years.

Until the end of the war, Dad was a combat radioman on the Pacific front. He spent an additional two years with the American forces occupying Japan. In early 1947, he came home. Within six months of his return, he dated and impregnated JoAnne Riley, his sister Cornelia's best friend and, later, my mother.

It was a game changer.

At the time, he was trying to rekindle his dream by playing baseball in a semi-pro league. Semi-pro paid nothing.

JoAnne (Riley) Matson and Emerson Nels Matson
at Snoqualmie Falls, 1947

After some soul-searching, he reluctantly put his baseball career aside and accepted his fate as JoAnne's husband and my father. He and JoAnne married January 10, 1948.

I was born May 17, 1948.

Now that he had a family to support, his priorities changed. Two things increasingly became his primary focus: his family and a desire to leave a positive legacy when his time on earth was up. For the latter, he chose to tell about the Battle of the Little Bighorn from the Native side. To become a writer as his Grandmother had suggested. The punishments he experienced for telling the truth at Camp Stoneham still burned inside him. However, just as the war had impeded his baseball career, life impeded fulfilling his chosen legacy.

In the late 1960s and early 1970s, Dad took two trips, each lasting about a week, to Lakota reservations in South Dakota. He listened to a few Lakota tribal elders tell their legend stories. On one visit to the Pine Ridge Reservation, he met an elder named Edgar Red Cloud. I remember him telling me that Red Cloud asked him for money to buy milk for his grandkids. When he obliged, Red Cloud sent his son to buy it from the local grocery. When he returned, his son only had a bag full of liquor. Red Cloud was embarrassed and apologized profusely to my father. My father accepted his apology.

Shortly afterwards, Red Cloud gifted him with some memorable legend stories. Then he gave my dad a Lakota name, "He Luta." In English it means "Red Horn."

My father wrote two books that included the legend stories Red Cloud and other Natives had given to him. However, his work schedule prevented him from spending any more time with Red Cloud or any other Lakota. Extra time that might have made them feel comfortable enough to tell their oral histories.

I believe Dad was unaware that they held back. All he knew was he had a family to feed and couldn't afford the cost of staying any longer than a week at a time. Soon thereafter, he took a job as an advertising executive that demanded most of his energy. As a result, he put his writing aside—for nearly thirty years.

Once diagnosed with lymphoma, however, with his mortality staring him in the face, distractions and procrastination were no longer an option. He sat down and started writing about the Lakota and Cheyenne side of the Battle of the Little Bighorn, fulfilling the vow he had taken as an army trainee at Camp Stoneham.

Chemotherapy treatment prevented him from visiting South Dakota. So without original stories from Lakota or Cheyenne, he got all his information from previously published sources.

During my visit to the hospital that day, Dad motioned for me to pull the curtain shut to give us privacy from his roommate. I did.

"Sit down," he said, gesturing to the chair beside his bed.

Whenever he asked me to sit down, it usually meant I was about to endure a boatload of advice on how I could improve my life. His advice always felt like criticism, even though he meant well.

I mentally circled the wagons and put on a brave front to prepare for hearing his "advice."

He looked me squarely in the eye and said, "I want you to do something for me."

I knew I had not been there for him for most of his life—not like my younger brother Bob, who had lived with our parents nearly his entire life. Bob was there whenever they needed a strong back. He was somebody they could depend on. I had avoided spending much time with my family—only holidays and special events. I rarely took the time to even call.

William, Mariellen, and Bob

My sister, Mariellen, was never shy about visiting him either. I felt I deserved his love the least of his three children. I expected and even hoped to be treated in a way that coincided with the way I felt about my past behavior. By granting his request, whatever it would be, I hoped to bring my guilt down to a manageable level.

I leaned in to hear what he had to say.

"I want you to finish my book."

His request caught me by surprise. I didn't believe myself to be a writer. Yet, this was the project closest to his heart, the legacy he wanted to leave behind. He had been writing night and day since he discovered his death was imminent. He now realized he wouldn't be able to finish it.

I felt unworthy. I had been the absent son. I didn't know what he had written or how far he had gotten. But I knew I could not say no.

This was a chance at redemption—if not in his eyes, in my own. I exploded into uncontrollable sobs of grief and gratitude. I would carry out this obligation with all my capabilities. That day changed my life once again, forever.

The next day I went back to Portland to polish off the post-production for my film and solicit prospective distributors. I crafted a letter and sent it with a copy of the movie to prospects. I waited two months for their replies and got none. While this was going on, I would check in with Dad to see how he was doing. Our conversations became shorter with each call. His energy was diminishing.

Then one day my mom called, and she asked me to come home.

It was time to bid him farewell.

As I stood next to his hospital bed and helplessly watched him writhe in pain. I didn't know if he could hear me. I spoke to him anyway. I reassured him I would finish the legacy he wanted to leave behind. I told him I would find a computer so I could put his manuscript in the proper format. Computers were not as commonplace in 1998 as they are today. I then turned to Mom and asked if I could borrow her computer, thinking to reassure Dad I was in earnest.

"No. I need it."

Her reply stunned me. Thoughts of losing her husband must have affected her thinking. But I needed my dad's life to end on a positive note.

Before I could find the words myself, Dad suddenly came to life. He pointed at me like a television pitch man, and exclaimed with all the authority of a man in full command of the room, "You got it!"

He turned to Mom and told her to make sure I got a computer.

That was the last time I would hear his voice. He then went back to spending all his energy trying to stay alive.

I stayed an hour more, and then I had to go. I kissed him on the forehead and walked out with tears rolling down my cheeks.

He died about a half hour later, on May 25, 1998. Two days after his seventy-second birthday.

I knew nothing about the Lakota or Cheyenne. I had always considered that to be my father's domain. But now his domain was my domain. The subject was miles outside my comfort zone, but it did not matter. I could not live with myself unless I fulfilled his dying wish.

Thus my journey into the world of our Native people began.

Chapter Three
The Search Begins

AFTER MY FATHER'S FUNERAL, I read his manuscript. It was apparent he was not healthy when he wrote it. Chemotherapy and contemplating his own death had robbed him of the concentration he needed to write a cohesive story.

He had been told previously by a book consultant that a book needed at least one hundred thousand words to be considered for publication. As I am now a published author, I know that is untrue. However, he believed it. And he used the last bits of his life to write one hundred thousand words. Yet for a book to be more than a vanity project, his words needed substance. Substance was lacking.

Writing books was foreign to me at the time. I felt more comfortable writing in a form I was familiar with—a film script. So that's what I did.

Simultaneously, I continued my efforts to get a distributor for my movie. One distributor I offered my film to was Miramax. After previewing my movie, one of their representatives called me. He spent an hour telling me what a splendid job I had done. He ended the conversation by telling me his boss, Harvey Weinstein, didn't like musicals, so they passed on my film. I got similar rejections from other distributors, except they sent form letters on exceptionally high-quality paper.

A year later, Weinstein was executive producer and his company, Miramax, the distributor for the film *Chicago*—a musical. So much for "Harvey didn't like musicals." Miramax had not been honest with me. However, by this point I was broke. So I turned the page. I shifted my focus to finishing my father's book.

My father wanted to tell the "Battle of the Little Bighorn" from the American Indian perspective. In deference to that, I paid a visit to the Little Bighorn Battlefield in Montana, to get a better feel for that story.

I hired a professional tour guide. He told me the generally-accepted story of the battle most people familiar with the event already knew—that Custer was one of the last men standing and how valiant he and his men had been. When I asked about the "Indian side" he told me there were people from the Crow Tribe he could introduce to me. However, the Crow fought on Custer's side, so I declined his offer.

To follow my father's vision, I needed to find Lakota or Cheyenne people that would tell me their family stories of the battle. I did not know anyone in the Plains states. However, my father hadn't known of Edgar Red Cloud before he boarded his plane for South Dakota. So I took a page from his life and sought to find my own Edgar Red Cloud.

I started up my computer, the one my father had granted me on his deathbed, and went onto the internet—still in its infancy in 1998.

Finding a Lakota or Cheyenne with an email address in those days was hard. The Lakota and Cheyenne reservations were among the poorest communities in the United States, and computers cost over a thousand dollars back then. I finally found a website listing a Northern Cheyenne tribal member named Eugene Little Coyote with an email. He worked at Dull Knife College, in information technology. The site listed his contact information, so after sending a quick introductory email I called and asked if he had any family stories about the Little Bighorn battle. He said he did, and I asked if I might come out and get them from him. He said yes.

I flew to Billings, Montana, rented a car, and drove to Lame Deer, Montana. Upon arriving at the college, I entered a building marked "administration" and asked for him. The receptionist at the front desk told me he was at lunch, but volunteered to take me to his office. As we entered his office, I found him eating his lunch. He was younger than I had pictured. He looked to be in his early thirties.

Upon seeing me enter, he stuffed the remains of his lunch in his desk drawer while the receptionist left to resume her duties.

I extended my hand, "I'm Bill Matson. I was the one that called you from Portland, asking about stories of the Battle of the Little Bighorn."

He stood, shook my hand, and seemed surprised I was there. His face turned stern.

"What kind of stories?"

"Stories that the elders passed down to you or that you might know," I replied.

"You mean like family stories?"

"Yes," I answered.

"I don't know any," he said coldly.

I was taken aback. This didn't match with what I understood from our phone conversation. However, I determined I was not going home empty-handed.

"Well, is there somebody else who might?" I asked.

"Follow me," he said as he exited from behind his desk and led me down a corridor. I followed eagerly, hoping he might lead me to an elder who knew some genuine stories of the battle. Maybe I would even hear stories that had never been told outside the Northern Cheyenne community. My heart beat with anticipation.

When we got to our ultimate destination, no one was there. Just rows of books on shelves. He had taken me to the Dull Knife College Library.

"Read these."

I looked at him as if to say, "This is it?"

He motioned to the books again.

"That's all I got." With that, Little Coyote turned and retreated to his office.

I stood in front of shelves full of books about the Plains Native people. I could have gotten these at any library or bookstore in Portland. I now realized fulfilling my father's last request would require a lot more effort than I had imagined.

Once I got home, I found an application for a credit card in my mailbox. I filled it out, and they issued me credit. I used it to buy about three hundred books on the Lakota, the Cheyenne, and even some on Custer.

One thing I learned from those books was that the Indians were not Indians, nor were they Native Americans. They were Natives. Native to Turtle Island, which is the Native name for North America. To show respect, I would refer to the Native Americans as Natives from that point on.

While reading the books, I concentrated on just the historical portions. I skipped anything having to do with Lakota or Cheyenne spirituality, deeming those parts not pertinent. After all, I had been in combat, and I had never once called on my time spent in church to dictate my actions. I figured the Lakota and Cheyenne were no different.

Most of the books about the history of the Plains Native people were written by purported "experts" who borrowed their information from other purported "experts." They wrote their books based on an interpretation of that borrowed information—like what my father had done at the end of his life. They rarely included authentic Native voices. The "experts" were almost always from non-Lakota cultures. Their conclusions never rang true to me.

One afternoon in early 1999, my mom called to ask if I would come with her, Bob, Mariellen, and their immediate families to Disney World in Orlando. A Caribbean cruise would follow that.

I had my own agenda and was now spending most of my time researching the Lakota and Cheyenne. I was also working a full-time job, selling computer memory chips (something that is no longer in wide use today), so I could eat. I told her that my siblings had kids and I didn't, so it made no sense for me to go to a Disney theme park or on a cruise. I told her to spend the money saved by my absence on her grandchildren.

She burst into tears. She begged me to come.

Hearing her cry made me realize how important it was to her. I never did find out *why* it was so important to her, but I had never experienced my mother so desperate for me to go somewhere with her my entire life. I relented.

She told me we would make the trip in February 1999, reasoning the Florida hurricane season would be over. I thought that an unusual basis for picking a date; after all, millions live in Florida all year round. But that was how Mom wanted it. She wanted our time together to be without complications.

When February came, our family gathered and flew to Florida. Once we arrived, my mom began complaining about a several-day-old episode she was having with constipation. She was experiencing severe cramps. She had not told us before our flight, because she didn't want us to worry. But now that we had landed, we were allowed to worry. The following morning she went to see a physician in the city of Celebration, just outside Orlando. The physician diagnosed her as having a cancerous tumor in her intestines which was blocking her bowel movements. She needed to have it removed immediately or lose her life. They operated that evening.

The next morning, while resting in the hospital, my siblings and I visited her. She told us she was all right and encouraged us to go on the Caribbean cruise.

"And leave you alone?" I exclaimed. "No way!"

She insisted.

I reasoned with her: since my siblings had children, it made sense that they and their families go on the cruise. I would stay back and monitor her recovery. Besides, she needed at least one family member to make sure she had a voice in case things went south. With that said, she agreed to allow me to stay.

Two days later, her doctors declared she would make a full recovery. However, they kept her in the hospital so she could heal. I slept on a padded bench in her room.

Two weeks later, my work called and asked me to please come back. By this time, my siblings had already flown home. So, I called my sister and asked her to replace me at the hospital. I needed to keep my income. She agreed, and I returned home. Another two weeks later, my sister brought Mom home.

Mom continued to recover at home over the next few months. She called occasionally to request I visit her. To entice me, she took a bigger interest in how I was handling my father's request to finish his book. To help, she offered to take me to the Black Hills, even though she was still taking chemo pills. Her offer was attractive. Going to the Black Hills would be helpful in learning about the Lakota and Cheyenne. After making sure her doctor said it was okay for her to travel, I accepted.

She bought our plane tickets for the second week of August 2000. However, when we tried to find a motel in Rapid City, South Dakota, nearly all were booked. When I questioned why rooms were so scarce, a motel clerk told us it was because of the Sturgis Rally.

The Sturgis Rally is the largest motorcycle rally in the world and falls on the second week of August. Hundreds of thousands of motorcyclists show up. Rapid City is only a few miles from its epicenter. Hence, nearly every room in western South Dakota was unavailable—even at double the normal price.

When we finally found a room, we booked it. Once we arrived, we found it difficult to sleep at night because of the constant roar of motorcycles riding through the motel parking lot at all hours. So we left Rapid City and headed east towards the Lakota reservations.

William and his mother, JoAnne, at Fort Abraham Lincoln's Hidatsu camp, 2000

Mom at a Pine Ridge Reservation Casino

Once on the reservations, my mom assumed command of our travel itinerary and made sure we stopped at all the Native casinos because, she said, she liked their buffets. However, in reality she had developed a fondness for the one-armed bandits. Although technically on a Lakota reservation, my spending so much time in casinos kept me from expanding my knowledge of the Lakota.

It was frustrating. I spent most of my time as a caretaker rather than researching.

We spent the last day of our trip at the Crow Fair in Crow Agency, Montana. The Crow Fair is one of the largest Native annual gatherings in North America. During the third week of August, it is the tipi capital of the world, with about fifteen hundred tipis. In addition, events included a powwow, rodeo, parade, and several feasts. Even though they had fought on Custer's side, I was curious to see what that many tipis in one place looked like.

During our visit, my mother waxed poetic about how great the Native people were. How they were misunderstood and suffered because of the poor treatment by our government. How they understood the Earth better than any other people, and how she wished to find some way to help them.

Then the clock struck noon: lunch time.

I asked her if she wanted to have one of the Indian tacos featured by one of the Native vendors. Maybe help them by purchasing a couple.

She gave me a disapproving stare and said out of the corner of her mouth, "I don't trust their food".

At that point, although I loved her, I knew she would never be helpful with the research I was doing for my dad. I needed to go on this journey for my dad alone.

After my return home, I saved my pennies for another trip to South Dakota. I still wanted to experience what my father had experienced.

Besides, there was a warrior I had learned of in my readings that piqued my interest.

His name was Crazy Horse.

Chapter Four

My Father Returns

IN THE SPRING OF 2001, I revisited the Black Hills.
A friend named Karen LaVoie asked to accompany
me. Even though I had vowed to go it alone, I was sweet
on her, and that sweetness won out. We rented a car at
the Billings Airport and drove to Custer State Park in the
Black Hills, arriving in the dark.

The cottage we rented was an old, Western-style log
cabin with a wooden wrap-around porch and a fireplace.
After the long drive, we fell right to sleep.

At sunrise, the morning mist rose around our cabin,
revealing a wonderland of life. Tall pine trees surrounded
us. A pair of white-tail deer grazed near the window. The
ground was lush with green vegetation and a brightly
colored rainbow of wild flowers flaunted their beauty. A
parade of bees frequented these flowers and rocked them
gently as they harvested the nectar. Everything was in per-
fect harmony.

I had read the Lakota regarded the Black Hills as
sacred. Upon reading the passage, I skipped forward to a

William stands by the cabin in Custer State Park, SD, 2000

more historically oriented section of the book. I did not want to read outside the lines of the culture I had grown up with and understood. But the unintentionally read text did not escape my memory. Now the passage came to life before my very eyes. The natural beauty and serenity of the Black Hills can only be described as sacred.

Once outside the cabin, I took in the fresh air and felt rejuvenated. I fell in love with the Black Hills that day. I wanted to know them better.

We took a tour to view the park's wildlife in an open-air jeep, soon encountering a small herd of about twenty buffalo, larger animals than I had pictured. They grazed along the roadside as though they hadn't a care in the world. Many were losing their winter coats. Large swaths of shedding fur swayed loosely as they walked, giving them a rather unkempt look. The patches where the furry winter coat had fallen off revealed a fresh, sleek, healthy fur underneath.

I learned from books that at one time the buffalo numbered in the millions and dominated the North American plains. When the Lakota and Cheyenne tribes roamed free, they derived everything needed to survive from these creatures. Now, their numbers were but a tiny fraction of what they once were.

We saw pronghorn, which the locals call antelope, racing across the prairies. They would watch us approach with curiosity, only to sprint away as our vehicle got closer. We spotted prairie dogs popping out of their burrows and scampering to fetch food, then sitting on their back legs to survey their surroundings before diving back into their burrows. There were colorful butterflies. Deer. Elk. Marmots. Chipmunks. Squirrels. Meadowlarks. Red-tailed hawks. Bighorn sheep. Bushy cottonwoods. Chokecherry bushes. Birch trees. Pine trees. And sparkling, clear water. Clear enough to see fish trolling for food beneath the water's surface. Paradise, as it was meant to be.

As fascinating and gorgeous as it was, I had to remind myself I wasn't learning anything about the Cheyenne and Lakota side of the Battle of the Little Bighorn.

I refocused.

At one of our stops, I came upon a brochure advertising a place called Crazy Horse Mountain, near Custer, South Dakota. It seemed like a logical place to learn about Crazy Horse, the warrior who had piqued my interest, so we went.

Crazy Horse Mountain is sculptor Korcak Ziolkowski's representation of Crazy Horse in the form of a gigantic rock carving. That day, their annual Volksmarch was taking place. The Volksmarch is an organized ten-kilometer hike up the mountain to the carving of Crazy Horse's face, which was the only thing carved in a recognizable form at the time. To increase participation, Crazy Horse Mountain offered free admission to all who joined the hike. Karen and I took part.

Following a brief tour of the facilities, I concluded this wasn't the place to learn about Crazy Horse. However, I found the magnitude of the Crazy Horse rock carving awe-inspiring. After taking photos of ourselves standing in front of Crazy Horse's face, Karen and I walked back to the car.

Still not having learned any new Lakota or Cheyenne stories about the Little Bighorn, I was again feeling frustrated.

So I made an unnatural decision for me. I would visit what I'd read was the Cheyenne and Lakota's most sacred

William with the carving of Crazy Horse in the background, 2000

William stands in front of
Crazy Horse face carving, 2000

of sites: Bear Butte. I was ready to venture outside my comfort zone, albeit for just a day.

We arrived at the sacred site the next morning. Geologically it is a volcano, formed by a surge of molten rock pushed upward to form a volcanic mountain that never erupted. I could not see its peak, 4,426 feet high, because of low-hanging clouds.

The weather was cooler than our previous days in the Black Hills, so we dressed a little warmer. Karen was excited to experience the spiritual nature of Bear Butte. She told me she was sure the mountain would give her an epiphany. I smiled and said nothing, not wanting to rain on her parade.

Upon entering the trailhead leading to the top of Bear Butte, we found ourselves surrounded by an abundance of colorful strips of cloth tied to the branches of trees and shrubs called prayer cloths. The cloths were red, blue, yellow, white, green, black—all the colors in the rainbow. Maybe I would learn something, after all.

As we started our climb, Karen, eager to get her epiphany, zoomed up the butte and out of sight. I did not keep up. I didn't feel the need and expected no epiphanies

William, with Bear Butte in the background, shrouded in clouds on the day of his climb

or visions. To me this was strictly a fact-gathering experience.

I was most curious to reach the top, anticipating that was where I would see what "spiritual" looks like to the Lakota and Cheyenne.

After a brief time, a steady rain fell. The clothes I wore became soaked. The trail became slippery. Portions of the trail were nothing more than a bed of loose rocks, which made the footing unsteady. I had worn a pair of low-cut tennis shoes. With no support for my upper ankles, I slid dangerously close to losing my

Beginning of Bear Butte trail to the top

balance more than once. I had to concentrate to keep from falling onto my backside.

As I struggled up the trail, I saw much of the mountain had been visited by a recent forest fire. Many of the trees were charred or burned. The beauty I had witnessed at the base became less inspiring the higher I hiked.

I was not in the best physical shape. The climb was exhausting. The continual upward ascent made my leg muscles burn. I thought about turning back, but masculine pride propelled me onward. I knew Karen would make it to the top, so I needed to be there, too.

As I continued to struggle, I rued the day I learned of Bear Butte. I had vowed not be sucked into examining Native spirituality in any way, shape, or form. "Shame on me for doing this," I scolded myself.

My cognitive powers waned, depleted by fatigue. I forced myself to focus on just putting one foot in front of the other. Without warning, on a straight, rocky stretch heading north on the eastern side of the butte, a little less than halfway through my climb—my father spoke to me.

Three years had passed since his death, but I heard his voice unmistakably. I looked around and I saw nothing unusual. But I knew it was him.

"Open your heart," he told me.

I understood his meaning immediately. Learning the Cheyenne and Lakota side of the Little Bighorn battle was not just about the battle. It was about all the things I had shied away from in my readings. Their way of life. Their spirituality. The Little Bighorn battle was just a single page from a much bigger book. I had to stop trying to learn about the Lakota and their ways through the tiny window

*William stands in the area on the Bear Butte trail where
his father told him, "Open your heart"*

of "history-only" readings. He wanted me to learn about
their ways through my heart.

Who fired what shot, and from where, had obscured
the bigger question of *why* it all happened. I was guilty of
tunnel vision. I dropped my prejudices against Lakota and
Cheyenne spirituality and embraced it.

Dad, too, had missed the boat on their spirituality.
However, wherever he went in death, he had learned
something. Fortunately for me, he had come back to share
that. Now anything that came out of this journey would
be ours, his and mine. He told me to open my heart—to
follow it, to tell its truth. What I produced now would
become both our legacies.

Hearing him gave me fresh energy. New life. My leg
muscles burned no more. About a half hour later, I neared
the top of the butte.

The wooden steps and platform at the butte's peak came into view. Huffing and puffing, I climbed the last thirty-four wooden steps. Once at the top, a cool breeze greeted me. The platform was a broad, thoroughly soaked, wooden deck. Resting climbers occupied the only two benches. A few small pine trees, adorned with prayer cloths, nestled just outside the deck. Karen sat cross-legged and meditating in one of the deck's corners.

The low cloud covering had cleared. A red-tailed hawk circled overhead, welcoming me to the summit. I could see the northern Black Hills to the southwest and the plains to the north, stretching for miles.

With no place to sit and exhausted, I laid down on the deck and stared into the sky. I was oblivious to the deck's shallow puddles soaking my clothing to a greater extent than it already was.

Platform at the top of Bear Butte

After an hour of allowing my experience to sink in, I headed back down with a new purpose. Karen joined me. She told me she had had the vision she wanted. I congratulated her, but maybe not with the gusto I should have. I was preoccupied with my revelation, which I hadn't expected, and I was still trying to digest it. I told her of my experience, but in the vaguest terms to avoid questions I could not answer.

I vowed I would go back to the books and find the sections I had skipped, because I now knew their culture and spirituality were pertinent, even essential.

Should I tell others what I experienced? If someone told me their dead father spoke to them while hiking up a butte, I would have dismissed them as a wacko.

Yet it had happened.

I wasn't ready to be lumped in with the wackos. So after telling Karen, I kept my mouth shut. Being comfortable to talk about it would come later.

I went home to read all the books I could find on Lakota spiritual ceremonies; not as much was published on Cheyenne ceremonies. Each book claimed their way of performing the ceremonies was the one and only way, yet each description differed from the others. I wondered how this could be.

I focused on the Lakota. I decided I would write about a single Lakota life that was steeped in their ways. The Lakota life that had most piqued my curiosity was Crazy Horse's. He would be the one I would concentrate on, to learn the bigger picture of the Lakota way of life and the reasons they had fought. Crazy Horse would be my script's centerpiece.

As I poured over the passages on spirituality I had skipped in my previous readings, I transferred those passage's meanings and descriptions directly into my film script. I wrote them in a painstakingly detailed fashion, researching everything, building a consensus of the similarities present from the differing ways the books described their ceremonies. I wanted my father to be proud. I wanted it to be accurate. To present a truth. To be the best thing I had ever done. I agonized over each sentence. Each phrase. Each word. Each ceremony description. It took me nearly a year to finish writing. Finally, I felt good about the script—except for one thing.

I did not know all the names of the people in Crazy Horse's life. Their names were not in any of the books. That made the story feel incomplete. I didn't know the names of the women who raised him after his birth mother, Rattling Blanket Woman, died when he was four years old. I learned he had a sister, but I didn't know her name either. Labeling people as important as the women who raised him and the woman he grew up with as stepmother #1 and #2 or sister #1 was just plain wrong.

Other than that, I knew I had something to present to a movie studio that they just might give me a green light to make. All I needed to do was give his sister and stepmothers names. If I learned their actual names, it would be a fitting tribute to my dad's desire for truth.

It had only been about three to four generations since Crazy Horse lived. That wasn't very long ago. I figured some Lakotas, three or four generations removed from him, could still be alive and would probably know their names.

I searched the internet once again for a new Lakota site or name since the last time I searched. I had nothing to lose. Then I found one.

Chapter Five
The Sweat Lodge

D AVID LITTLE ELK'S WEBSITE had what I was looking
for. He had written a book on Lakota spirituality and
way of life, plus one on the Lakota language.

I ordered the Lakota spirituality book. Even though
quite overpriced, I wanted to learn as much as possible.

Little Elk was a Lakota from the Cheyenne River Reservation in South Dakota. I had read about Pine Ridge,
Rosebud, and Standing Rock Reservations, but very little
about Cheyenne River.

After buying and reading his book, I developed a
rapport with Little Elk via email. I asked him about
Crazy Horse's stepmothers and sister. He said he was
aware of some people on the Cheyenne River Rez (slang
for reservation) who knew the women's names, and he
might put me in touch with them. Excited, I wanted to
meet him and these people.

To work around my job, I needed a long weekend
where I could have an extended visit with Little Elk.
The three-day Memorial Day weekend fit the bill. He

confirmed Memorial Day weekend would suit him also. So I packed my script in with my flight luggage, to see what he thought.

Once in Rapid City, I drove over two hours to the city of Faith, where I stayed at the Prairie Vista Inn Motel. Faith borders the Cheyenne River Reservation. Once I settled at the motel, I called him.

A woman answered and told me he was at a powwow. (A powwow is a Native celebration of dance and music).

"A powwow? When is he due back?" I queried.

"Probably tonight."

I told her we were scheduled to meet and asked her to take a message for him to call as soon as possible. She said she would.

I waited until dusk for a call, but none came. I called again and was told he still wasn't there. I left another message.

Dusk turned to night. I called again. Nobody picked up. I tried again after 9:00 p.m., and still no answer.

I called the next morning and the same woman said she didn't think he would be home for the rest of the weekend.

Disappointed, I swore I wouldn't spend my remaining two days in my motel room. I drove to Bear Butte. Maybe my father had another message.

Once I arrived, I entered the Bear Butte State Park's visitor center. I hadn't done that on my first visit.

A Native lady park ranger greeted me. I told her I wanted to learn about the Lakota, specifically their spirituality and way of life. I also mentioned my quest for Crazy Horse's sister's and stepmothers' names.

She suggested I talk to Jim.

Bear Butte

"Jim?"

"I'll go get him," she replied. She disappeared into another room.

I thought I had the right person. She was Native, and because of geographical location, most likely a Lakota. Now I was waiting for somebody I hoped wasn't a non-Native government worker, telling me things I could read off a brochure.

She reappeared with Jim Jandreau, the head ranger, who, much to my relief, was also Native. He extended his hand.

He seemed friendly, so I repeated what I told the woman and even mentioned my script.

In the middle of my spiel, his eyes lit up.

"I got something for you." Then he disappeared.

When he returned, he handed me a scrap of paper with a telephone number on it.

"This is Doug War Eagle's number. He's a member of the Crazy Horse family. He can set you straight."

I couldn't believe my ears. A member of the Crazy Horse family? This phone number seemingly came straight from heaven. Maybe Dad was sending help, one more time.

Ecstatic, I thanked him profusely and told him I'd call Doug as soon as I got to a place with cell phone service (in 2002, Bear Butte had no cell service).

As I left, Jim called out to advise me to bring Doug tobacco, as a sign of respect. Then he disappeared into his office.

Meanwhile, as I passed the woman park ranger on my way out, I thanked her, and I asked if I should bring Doug War Eagle anything extra if he agreed to meet.

"Bring something useful," she said. "Like food."

On my drive back, I thought how proud my father would have been for me getting the Crazy Horse family's contact information. I relished the thought I might hear the Lakota stories that eluded him.

Then a fresh fear entered my brain. Could this be too good to be true?

I began guarding against my own optimism.

Upon reaching my motel, I took out my cell phone to dial Doug's number. Halfway through dialing, I stopped.

A worried voice spoke from inside my head. "Doug doesn't know me. Why would he even want to talk to me? What do I have to offer?"

I put the phone down. I went to bed, but even in bed my mind wouldn't stop racing. I did not sleep that night.

The next morning, I agonized over whether to call him all over again.

I fidgeted. I paced.

I couldn't stay still.

What would I say if he answered the phone?

By late afternoon, with my long weekend nearly over, I finally overcame my fears and called him. I owed it to my father.

Doug answered. My heart skipped a beat.

I nervously introduced myself, and mentioned Jim Jandreau suggested I call.

Doug spoke in a warm and welcoming tone. His humbleness calmed my nerves. He told me he knew Jim was a good man and he would see me. "You'll also meet two of my brothers," he said. Then he ended the conversation by giving directions to his place.

I was relieved. Jubilant. I had a meeting with members of the Crazy Horse family. I felt my father smiling from above.

I wanted Doug and his brothers not to regret their decision to see me. Remembering what the park rangers said, I jumped in my car and sped to the grocery store. I bought steaks, orange juice, watermelon, potatoes, fresh vegetables, coffee, and other goods, along with tobacco.

After stopping by my motel and grabbing my script, I drove to meet them.

During my drive, I alternated between cloud nine and the pessimistic thought they wouldn't find any value in working with me.

My mind exploded with scenarios and strategies. What if they didn't like my movie script? I got to thinking I could suggest writing a book as a backup plan, which had been my dad's original medium of choice—not really my comfort zone, but better than going home empty-handed.

Doug's place was about twenty miles east of Faith, near Dupree, South Dakota. I arrived at a small, bluish-gray, simple single-story home.

With butterflies in my stomach and tobacco in hand, I knocked on his door.

A Native man who looked to be in his early forties opened the door. He wore glasses and had neatly trimmed black hair. He was younger than I expected.

"Doug War Eagle?"

"That's me," he replied with a smile.

I introduced myself. He told me they had been expecting me. "The grandfathers told us you were coming."

"Grandfathers?"

"Our grandfathers. They told us you would come from the west."

I had indeed come from the west, but I mentally dismissed his knowledge of me as just Little Elk spreading the word of my arrival, prior to standing me up.

Doug invited me into his home and introduced me to his brother Floyd Clown. Floyd looked to be in his late thirties or early forties. I assumed he was Doug's younger brother. Later I found he was actually Doug's eldest brother. He also wore glasses and had long, thick, black hair tied into a ponytail.

Doug then introduced me to Kevin Dyda. Kevin's full head of long, light-brown hair, matched a skin tone several shades lighter than everybody else's in the room but mine. I learned Keven had spent nearly his entire life in the military and recently moved to the rez from North Carolina.

Floyd said Kevin had come from the east. "He's the one writing our book on Crazy Horse from what the family knows."

My heart sank, because that meant I had just lost my backup plan.

I soldiered on.

"Cool, so east meets west," I joked, as I shook Kevin's hand.

"Our grandfathers told us you were coming from the west four days ago. They said help would come from all four directions. Our lawyers who are helping us to claim our Crazy Horse estate in Rosebud Tribal Court came from the south. We're still waiting on the one from the north," Doug explained.

I believed nothing good would come from discussing court appearances—at least not on our initial meet. I focused on making a favorable impression.

I turned to the book writer, "So you're the one writing their book?"

Kevin nodded proudly.

"How far along are you?"

"Just starting," Doug interjected.

"We have to visit some places," added Kevin.

"What do you mean?" I asked.

Doug elaborated by saying they needed to visit and get a feel for the places their grandfathers and grandmothers had told them about. That way they could authenticate and verify their oral history before telling it to others. (The Lakota had no written language. Their history passed from generation to generation orally.)

"Have you been to most of the places already?" I queried.

"We been to some, but there are more we need to see," Doug replied.

"Can I go with you on one of your trips?" I asked.

Doug and Floyd exchanged a quick glance before Doug demurred, "We'll see."

I had hoped for yes, but at least they didn't say no.

Then Bentley In The Woods stepped forward. He introduced himself as Doug's uncle. He was thin, with the deep lines of life etched in his face. He looked to be in his late fifties or early sixties. He wore glasses. After we shook hands, he stepped back to allow Doug to resume our conversation.

"This is for you guys," I said handing Doug the tobacco. They thanked me and shook my hand in appreciation. Then I remembered the groceries in the car.

"I brought something for you guys. Is it okay if I go get it?" I asked.

Amused glances circulated the room. Finally, Doug smiled and simply said, "Go ahead."

I sprinted out to the car to retrieve the groceries. I also grabbed my script.

Seeing the groceries, they seemed surprised and pleased. They took turns thanking me for the food. Doug suggested we have the steaks later, but first they wanted to talk.

They ushered me to the dining room table and offered me a chair at the foot of the table. I sat down, script in hand.

Scattered coffee mugs and ashtrays filled with cigarette butts populated the table. I found Doug's home, other than his kitchen table, to be tidy.

"Do you want some coffee?" Doug asked.

I didn't need to be any more amped than I already was, but I also wanted to be polite. So I said yes. He poured me a cup.

Doug sat to my right. Floyd sat right across from me at the head of the table. Kevin sat in between Doug and Floyd, while Bentley leaned back against a kitchen counter behind Doug and Kevin, cradling a cup of coffee.

We smiled awkwardly at each other. Then Doug spoke, "So how do you know Jim?"

"I don't. I just told him about my script on Crazy Horse and how I was trying to find the names of Crazy Horse's stepmothers and sister. I also mentioned I wanted to learn more about the ways of your people. Then he got your phone number and gave it to me. Told me to call."

Kevin queried, "What are you talking about? A movie script?"

"Yeah, I got it here if you want to see it," I responded eagerly.

"Yup, I'd like to look," requested Floyd.

I handed it to Floyd, who thumbed through it as I told of my attempts to meet with Little Elk.

Doug interrupted, "He's a relative of ours."

"Really? He never told me that," I replied.

"That's good. He's not authorized to speak for our family," Doug stated.

I followed the Little Elk narrative with the story about my father being in the 7th Cavalry and how I was trying to fulfill his dying wish. I also told them about my dad getting a Lakota name and that someday I would like one, too.

"We can help. We were just at Bear Butte a few days ago, fixing up our grandmother's grave," Doug said. "And we have some stories."

"Stories? Cool. You have a grandmother buried at Bear Butte? Isn't that a state park?"

"Yeah, but it doesn't really belong to South Dakota. Bear Butte is within of our Nation. It belongs to our people. They buried our grandmother Good Looking Woman there. She's one of the women who helped raise Crazy Horse the warrior after his birth mother, Rattling Blanket Woman, killed herself. She was Rattling Blanket's older sister—probably one of the mothers you're looking for," Doug said with a twinkle in his eye.

"Yes! Good Looking Woman. Thank you." I said committing her name to memory. "And his birth mother killed herself?"

Doug nodded.

"Why?"

"Rattling Blanket was barren after giving birth to Crazy Horse. Then her husband, Waglula, brought home some new wives who might give him children. She didn't feel good about that, so she hung herself." Doug answered.

A brief, sobering silence followed.

"So how are you related to Crazy Horse?"

"We're the grandsons," Doug said proudly.

"I didn't think Crazy Horse had any children that lived to have kids."

"He didn't. His only child was a daughter, and she died as a toddler. We're direct from his father, Old Man Crazy Horse. They also called him Waglula or Worm," Doug explained.

"You're a grandson or a great grandson to Old Man Crazy Horse?" I asked.

They replied they were grandsons. There was no such thing as great grandsons or great granddaughters in their culture. They said the adjective "great" was a European thing.

Don Red Thunder, Floyd Clown, and Doug War Eagle

Doug and Floyd used their hands a lot as they spoke. I found it fascinating and told them so.

"Our grandmother Amy's dad couldn't hear too well, so we all learned to use our hands to help him out," Doug answered.

"And how did Good Looking Woman get her name?" I asked.

"She was good looking. Very beautiful." Doug answered. And then for further emphasis he added, "She was like—hot, or in other words, a ten-out-of-ten," which he followed with a nervous laugh.

"And the other woman that helped raise Crazy Horse?" I inquired.

"They Are Afraid Of Her. She was also Good Looking Woman's younger sister."

"I thought that was Crazy Horse's daughter's name."

"That's right. They named his daughter after his aunt. Crazy Horse wanted his daughter to be independent like her, so he gave her the same name."

"This is really informative," I said, beaming inwardly. "What about his sister's name?"

Doug paused. Then answered, "He didn't have a sister."

"I read he did."

"Nope.

Suddenly Floyd tossed my script into the middle of the table in disgust.

"Nothing in here is the truth. It's fiction. It's no good." He scowled.

My euphoria rapidly disappeared like a scrap of meat tossed to a pack of hungry wolves.

"What do you mean?" I asked, trying to hide how deeply he wounded me. I had done my homework. This was the best work I had ever done, and the only vehicle remaining that might enable me to spend more time with them.

"You have in here Crazy Horse is an Oglala. He was Minikouju. As soon as I saw that, I knew that there is no truth in your script. If you want the true story, you need to throw this away and start fresh with what we know."

I knew Oglala and Minikouju were two different bands within the Lakota Nation. But I had constructed my script in the same manner my father constructed his manuscript, by taking information from books by people I had never met.

"Where did you get the story from?" asked Floyd.

"Books I read."

"You wasted your time. Do you want the truth?" Floyd countered.

"Yeah, I do," I answered sheepishly.

"Then forget about this," he said, pointing at my script. "Forget about the books. Books don't know nothing about Crazy Horse or our family. The books are all written on assumptions."

I wasn't sure how to react. Starting over seemed impossible to even contemplate. But somehow, after taking a deep breath, I opened my mouth and out came, "So if I start over, will you tell me your family's stories about Crazy Horse and the Lakota?"

If I start over—just saying those words made my heart sink.

"We will, if you prove your heart to be good," Floyd answered.

I tensed up. How could I prove my heart was good?

I got my answer immediately.

Kevin hunched forward in a menacing way and said, "I challenge you to a sweat."

A sweat is where water is poured over red hot rocks to make steam in a non-porous, tent-like domed lodge. I had read the steam purifies everyone inside the lodge.

"A sweat lodge?" I asked eagerly.

"Yeah, a sweat lodge. I challenge you. I want to see if you can handle being cooked alive," Kevin answered with a smirk.

I had wanted to take part in a sweat lodge ceremony ever since I read about it. Now the opportunity materialized. But I didn't know if Kevin was kidding or not. I hadn't known him long enough. I figured that providing we all went in together, I wouldn't cook any more than he did. At least that's what I hoped.

Suddenly Doug's front door burst open. It was their younger brother, Don Red Thunder. After introducing ourselves to each other, he struck me as more outgoing than his brothers. Looking to be in his mid-thirties, he had long, flowing, thick black hair tied into a ponytail. Doug and Floyd updated him on our conversation, including that I had written a script with no truth, my desire for a Lakota name, and that we were planning to sweat.

Don turned to me, "So you want a Lakota name? Our family don't give those out easily."

"I understand." I then asked the question weighing most on my mind. "We're all sweating together, right? I'm not going to be in there by myself, am I?" I wanted to make sure Kevin was kidding.

"As a matter of fact, we are going to throw you in by yourself to see if it's safe," Don chuckled.

I turned pale.

Then he added with a teasing grin, "Aiiii, we'll all be in there together."

My hosts burst into laughter. An embarrassed smile creased my face.

Once the laughter died down, a seriousness crept into the room.

Floyd spoke. "We need to hear you pray. That way we can tell if you have a good heart."

It had been a long time since I last prayed. Not since Dad's funeral. But my desire to learn the truth about Crazy Horse overrode any apprehensions I had about praying.

"Okay, let's do it."

Doug's back door squeaked again. Don quickly got up to escort an older Native woman into the house. Everybody got quiet. Don introduced her as his and Doug's mother, Beverly Clown. I stood up and smiled. I was about to shake her hand when she shot me a look that would scare the feathers off a bird. She obviously didn't trust me.

If I hadn't known gaining the family's trust would be hard before, I did now.

We ended up shaking hands, but her body language told me shaking my hand wasn't her first choice.

"I was just agreeing to sweat with your sons," I said, trying to reassure her.

She nodded coldly, turned to Don, and asked to be escorted away.

"She only wanted to meet you," Don said apologetically, as he ushered her out.

"Nice to have met you!" I called after her as she exited. Silence greeted my words. My confidence took a hit.

I re-ignited my conversation with the brothers and Kevin, "Where is your sweat lodge, anyway?"

"Over at Floyd's," came the answer.

"Shall we go?" Doug asked. I nodded yes.

And with that, Doug made a quick trip to the refrigerator and grabbed the steaks I had brought.

We got into our respective cars, and I followed them to Floyd's.

Floyd lived in an off-white ranch house at the top of a long, dirt, rutted driveway.

The sweat lodge was in his backyard, along with Kevin's living quarters, a big canvas tipi.

Archival photo of uncovered sweat lodge

Weathered pieces of canvas and old carpets covered the dome-shaped sweat lodge. The opening faced to the west. A small mound of dirt, which they referred to as an altar, sat a few feet in front of the opening. A few more feet to the west, a large pit contained a layer of spent ashes.

I asked Floyd, who took charge of preparing the sweat, if the fire to heat the rocks would happen in the pit. I had gathered as much from my readings. He confirmed it was.

Then he explained the ceremony further, "When we go in the sweat, we breathe the Creator's air. We bring hot rocks, which represent fire and our Mother Earth, into the sweat lodge and place them in the center. We pour water on the rocks, which mixes with the air to create steam. That way we have all the elements of the Creator. Fire. Water. Earth. Air. All mixed to make the Creator's air."

Floyd showed me the rocks they would use. He called them lava rocks because they formed through volcanic activity. He said they preferred them, because they didn't split or crack when they got hot. There was also a pile of cut logs and tree limbs nearby, which were used to build and feed the fire that heated the rocks.

Floyd began preparations for our ceremony. He stacked the larger logs neatly in the pit to build a base for a fire. He then stacked several lava rocks on top of the logs. Seeing the others bring him the rocks, I joined in and helped.

After we gathered enough rocks for the sweat, I noticed everyone began bringing him wood. So I collected wood, too. Once I brought him my first load of wood, I got swept up in my enthusiasm and suddenly I couldn't bring him wood fast enough. I ran for more wood. Then my run turned into a sprint.

Floyd arranged the wood I brought all around the rocks in a tipi-like shape. My zeal in helping bring the wood to build the fire caused my hosts to give pause. Their eyes followed my every move.

"This guy kind of scares me," I overheard Bentley say to Floyd. My enthusiasm may have been a little over the top, but it was an honest response to the opportunity presented to me.

Once Floyd lit the fire, it was only a few minutes before it was a full-fledged bonfire. As we sat by the fire waiting for the rocks to heat, the family members and Kevin schooled me on what to know for my first sweat.

"If it gets too hot for you, just lie down. That's where the cooler air is, down by the ground," Don offered.

Doug suggested, "There's little pieces of sage scattered on the floor of the sweat. Just pick some up and hold it by your mouth and nose while you breathe, and it will cool you down."

Kevin gave a different scenario. He said I would come out looking like a cooked and blistered lobster. I called silently to the spirit of my dad to join me in the lodge and give me courage.

They instructed me to say "Mitakuye Oyasin" as I entered and exited the sweat lodge. It was a Lakota greeting to everything that populates Mother Earth and beyond. It means "we are all related." Everything on earth and in the sky is a relative to the Lakota. They are all part of the oneness and harmony of Creation.

They also said I could say "Mitakuye Oyasin" if it got too hot and needed the door opened.

I practiced saying it out loud. Gales of laughter met my awkward pronunciation. For much of the rest of our wait for the rocks to heat, Doug and Don coached me on how to say it properly. It didn't come easily for me.

Floyd informed me after the sweat, we would smoke and pray with his sacred pipe. He said the smoke from it would carry our prayers to all places so the Creator would know what prayer we carried in our hearts.

By late afternoon, the stones were red hot. Don, Floyd and Kevin planted their personal staffs deep into the dirt altar so they stood upright. Many eagle feathers and a wide swath of red cloth embellished Don's staff. It was beautiful and ornate. He said a friend had made it for him. Floyd's and Kevin's consisted of unadorned branches of wood, with their spiritual medicines attached.

Floyd loaded his pipe with tobacco while Don beat a hand drum with a padded drum stick and sang a Lakota song. We all stood with our hats off out of respect for the pipe being loaded. Even though I did not understand the words in their song, I understood the significance and gravity of just being there.

Once the song and pipe filling finished, we disrobed and entered the sweat lodge. Each of us said "Mitakuye Oyasin" as we entered. The floor of the sweat lodge was cool, damp, hardened dirt sprinkled with sage leaves. I sat between Doug and Kevin. Bentley stayed outside.

After we were all seated, Bentley carried the glowing, red-hot rocks, balanced on the prongs of a pitchfork, from the fire into the sweat lodge. He placed them into a small shallow pit in the center of the lodge. The rocks lit up and warmed the lodge immediately.

I drew my legs close to my body to keep my feet from touching the igneous rocks. Next to the lodge opening sat Floyd, with a large, hollow buffalo horn and a big, white plastic tub filled with water.

After Bentley finished delivering the rocks, dried flat cedar, sweetgrass and sage were sprinkled on them. The sprinklings instantly crackled and burned to a crisp. Then the opening to the lodge was closed and the only light came from the intense glow of the rocks.

Floyd filled his buffalo horn from the tub and slowly poured the water onto the rocks. They sizzled and hissed as the water cascaded over them and dimmed their glow. The steam that resulted slammed into my lungs and rocked me to my core. I breathed shallower for fear that my lungs might get burned.

Because it was my first time, it was difficult to judge how hot a temperature I would have to endure. However, I determined to last the entire ceremony without lying down or breathing with sage next to my mouth. I wanted to show my heart was not only a good heart, but a strong one, too.

Don brought his hand drum into the sweat lodge. He kept the beat as they sang three songs in Lakota. Floyd continued to pour water over the rocks while they sang. Not knowing the words to the songs, I just listened and bobbed my head to the beat.

Once they finished their third song, Floyd shouted "Mitakuye Oyasin." Bentley opened the sweat lodge door in response. The cool air from outside gave us immediate relief from the heat. They asked how I was managing.

"Good," I answered. My lungs had adapted, and I now enjoyed the Creator's air. My fears of a grueling endurance test disappeared.

Floyd explained they would close and open the sweat lodge door three more times for four times altogether, which would be the full length of the ceremony.

With that said, the door closed. The second round went much like the first round. More steam and three more Lakota songs. By the middle of the second round, my body and lungs had completely adapted to the heat.

It was wonderful.

When the second round ended and the door opened, Bentley brought in the rest of the rocks from the fire. Floyd said in the third round, I would say my prayer, in English. Theirs would be spoken in Lakota. Prayers would be said in a clockwise progression, so I would say mine after Kevin. The cue was to listen for him to say "Mitakuye Oyasin." All prayers ended with that phrase.

Don said his prayer first. Kevin followed. When Kevin said, "Mitakuye Oyasin," it became my turn.

I thanked the Creator for the opportunity to sweat with my new friends and asked Him to look after them and their families. I also asked He look after my family as well. Finally, I prayed for everyone on Mother Earth to have a better life. Then I said "Mitakuye Oyasin."

Doug prayed next. Then Floyd.

Finally, upon finishing their prayers, the door opened and then closed for the fourth and final round. They sang three more Lakota songs.

As the fourth round ended, Floyd emptied the rest of the water from the big white tub over the rocks. It gave us a final extreme rush of heat. Then he shouted, "Mitakuye Oyasin." Bentley opened the door, and it was over.

We exited the sweat lodge saying "Mitakuye Oyasin." Our sweat-drenched bodies met the cool evening air. It felt great. The ceremony had lasted over two hours. We used our towels to dry off and got dressed.

As we stood in a circle near the opening of the sweat lodge, Floyd lit his pipe. His pipe had a simple, red pipe-stone bowl connected to about a foot-long wooden stem.

We passed it around clockwise. Each one of us took a few puffs while saying a silent prayer of thanks.

After we finished smoking the pipe, we shook hands and thanked each other for the shared experience. Then we all went inside Floyd's house, except for Kevin. He went to his tipi to cook the steaks. He had a barbecue grill inside his tipi. When he finished cooking them, he brought them inside the house. We ate them in near silence.

The sweat lodge experience left me very refreshed and relaxed. However, I still didn't know their verdict on my heart. Their silence on the subject was deafening.

With no indications of how my heart stood, I spoke from the heart, "I wished I knew your language, I would have sung with you."

No one spoke for the longest time.

Finally, Bentley broke the silence, "They don't allow me to sweat with them because I end up singing Merle Haggard." (Merle Haggard was a popular country music singer.)

His unexpected response melted my anxiety into uncontrollable laughter. Bentley's comment told me, albeit unorthodoxly, that they accepted me. My heart had made the grade.

At least, that's what I thought.

Chapter Six

A Visit From The Wakiyans

WE CONTINUED TALKING AT Floyd's into the early morning.

"What places do you still need to see?"

"Slim Buttes," Kevin answered.

Slim Buttes is in the northwest corner of South Dakota, near the city of Reva.

"It's where our grandmother is lying," Don added.

When I asked which grandmother, Doug told me, "They Are Afraid Of Her."

"I'd pay for the gas if I come with you," I offered.

They greeted my request with silence. So, I continued, "How do you know that she's there?"

"You ask too many questions. Patience. Be patient," Floyd scolded.

"I really want to come," I persisted.

"We'll let you know," Doug replied.

I had no choice but to be patient. With sunrise fast approaching, I left for my motel.

Finally, the time came to go to the airport. Once onboard the plane, I reflected on all that had happened. I wondered what was so important about the court case they mentioned. To get into their good graces I had stayed with pleasant topics. Now I regretted not probing. I had left an important piece of the puzzle behind.

When I got home, I checked my emails. To my surprise, there was one from David Little Elk, saying Floyd, Doug, and Don were only after my money. Apparently he knew that we had met. Yet Little Elk charged an exorbitant price for his books, and he didn't show up or send a message that he would not meet me. On the other hand, I didn't really know Floyd, Doug, and Don that well, either. But at least they met and shared their time and culture without charge. That outweighed anything Little Elk had done. My gut told me it was better to trust Floyd, Doug, and Don.

Those back home that knew of my recent trip were curious. Karen was one of them. I told her about the privilege I had of meeting with members of the Crazy Horse family. And the supreme let down of having my script rejected. Now I needed to find someone I could borrow a video camera from so I could pitch their family on a documentary. That might be the only way of learning their story.

"All the people I know with professional video cameras would probably ask for big money," she stated.

"Yeah, well, that's something I don't have."

At my job, I found I could not concentrate. I would rather be fulfilling my father's dying wish. I wanted to know the Crazy Horse family's stories. Patience, for me, was elusive. I finally broke down and called Doug to ask if I could come visit again. For a few days.

William, 2004
Photo by Mark Frethem

Doug, 2004
Photo by Mark Frethem

He said he'd talk it over with his brothers and let me know.

I waited impatiently. A few days later, I called Doug to see what he and his brothers had decided. He told me they could meet and for me to name a time. We decided on the middle of July.

My search for a video camera resulted in finding one of my father's old still cameras, tucked away in a closet where it had been gathering dust for years. At least I'd be able to capture *some* images.

Once I arrived, Doug greeted me with the same warmth as he had previously. Floyd and Don were not available that day. After exchanging niceties, I asked him to explain the tribal court situation he had talked about the last time we met.

He informed me they faced two rival claims to the Crazy Horse estate. One was Seth Big Crow, from the Rosebud Reservation. The other was from the Pine Ridge Reservation. I learned later that claim belonged to a Pine Ridge enrolled member named Harvey White Woman.

An entity named the Crazy Horse Defense Project brought suit in federal court against the Hornell Brewing Company of Brooklyn, NY, for naming one of their liquors after Crazy Horse without permission from his family. They had called it Crazy Horse Malt Liquor. The Defense Project was the brainchild of True Clown, a Crazy Horse family relative, and his friend Big Crow. However, True Clown died before they formulated their fundraising efforts, leaving Big Crow as the sole administrator of the Defense Project. Any awards deemed prudent by the court would go to the Crazy Horse estate.

While raising money to cover the Defense Project's legal and court fee expenses, Big Crow represented himself as a Crazy Horse family member. This made Floyd, Doug, Don, and the rest of their family angry. They knew he was not a family member.

Some making and distribution of the malt liquor was sub-contracted to the G. Heileman Brewing Company, another named party in the lawsuit. The Strohs Brewing Company subsequently purchased G. Heilmann Brewing. Strohs then settled their inherited portion of the lawsuit by awarding the Crazy Horse estate with a letter of apology for using the Crazy Horse name, plus 32 Pendleton Blankets, 32 braids of sweet grass, 32 tobacco ties, and seven thoroughbred horses. They presented the entire package to Big Crow in 2001, thus eliminating Strohs from the lawsuit. Later, the lawsuit against the Hornell Brewing was also decided in favor of the Crazy Horse estate. The court's award this time was monetary.

Currently, the foremost question before the court was: Who were the rightful heirs of the Crazy Horse estate? Who should receive the award? The federal court delegated that question to the Rosebud Tribal Court on the Rosebud Reservation.

Thus the whole situation turned into a battle over who could prove in a court of law they were related to Crazy Horse.

Big Crow had raised several thousand dollars for the Crazy Horse Defense Project. However, there were rumors some of that money was allegedly being spent for Big Crow's personal use, which brought anxieties to Floyd, Doug, Don, and their legal counsel, Cheryl Bogue.

"My family is only claiming what's rightfully ours, because Big Crow's lawsuit has Crazy Horse's name attached," said Doug.

"Why don't people know you're the rightful heirs?"

"For generations, our grandfathers and older family members told us to keep their relationship with Crazy Horse quiet, because the government was looking for us—our lives were still in danger.

"Why did you think the government wanted to kill you?" I asked.

"We had family members killed at Wounded Knee in 1890, including Crazy Horse's first cousin, Bigfoot, who we knew as Spotted Elk. Then we had another relative, Peter Wolf (Makah), murdered by the government in 1918, after he said he was Crazy Horse's brother. After that, our grandmother was hunted in the 1930s after she had a letter written to say Crazy Horse was not buried on the Pine Ridge Rez, to repudiate a book that said he was. The government taught us it was best to be silent.

"All that changed in 2000, when the grandfathers learned the government changed their way of thinking and were no longer interested in killing us. So they released us from our vow of silence. Now the grandfathers want us to stand up and tell the truth."

"What are these grandfathers' names?" I asked.

Doug hesitated, and then said, "Just grandfathers."

Doug continued to say that once the courts declared them the legal heirs, they would claim the agency promised to Crazy Horse prior to his assassination in 1877, which was 8.7 million acres, including the Black Hills.

I asked, "What happens to the people living in the Black Hills today? They have homes there. What if they don't move off?"

"It's the government's responsibility to move them off. The government is the one that allowed them to be there," Doug responded.

I wondered privately if they could really pull this off. Who were these grandfathers that were advising them? I had yet to meet them.

The following day I visited Floyd. He was building a new sweat lodge from chokecherry branches and colored strips of cloth in his backyard. An ex-Lakota drum group singer, Butch Brown, was helping him. (A drum group consists of singers of Native songs while sitting around a large drum and beating a steady beat with padded drumsticks). I also noticed Kevin's tipi was gone. They said he had found his own place.

The sweat lodge they were building was more than double the size of the one I had sweated in. Floyd called the new sweat lodge a Bear Lodge, because it was for healing. In the Lakota way of living, the bear is an animal helper that brings healing. When a bear gets sick, he finds a root or herb to eat that will make him well. The Lakota learned of these roots and herbs by following a sick bear and noting the plants he selected. The Lakota then learned that this same root or herb could also heal their own people.

The lodge's opening faced to the east, not the west. Floyd told me the west is where the thunder beings come from, and that meant those sweats were to be run in a stricter way. For instance, English could not be spoken in them.

"Why did I get to speak English?" I asked.

"We allowed it because we needed to hear and understand your prayer, to see into your heart better. The grandfathers told me to build this new sweat lodge because the entire Lakota Nation will sweat with our family," Floyd proclaimed.

Although the new sweat lodge was much larger than the old one, I could not see how the entire Lakota Nation could fit in it unless they sweated in endless shifts.

"When did the grandfathers tell you this?"

Floyd sighed and said, "You ask too many questions," as he pushed the cut ends of the long chokecherry branches into the earth, placing them in such a way as to form a circle.

He next bent the branches he had anchored into the ground towards the center of the circle to form a dome shape. He tied them together at the top with the colored strips of cloth. Once tied, it established the shape of the sweat lodge.

Fascinated, I went to retrieve my camera. When I returned and began lining up my shots, Floyd objected, "Your pictures won't turn out."

"Why?" I queried.

"Our sweat lodge is sacred. I don't think the grandfathers will like you taking pictures of it," he answered.

I really didn't want superstition to prohibit some exceptional photo opportunities. I told him I wanted to try it, anyway.

Though unhappy about my insistence, Floyd allowed me to proceed. As I took the pictures, I noticed the lever on my camera was not advancing the film properly. It was slipping. I had not tested it before I came. However, my pride kept me from saying anything was wrong, lest he would say he told me so. The camera hadn't been used since long before my father's death, and not advancing the film properly may have been the reason.

After a while Floyd ran out of the strips of colored cloth and had to stop so he could make some more. While he was making them, Butch asked if I would like to get to know the rez better. I told him yes. So he and I went on a road trip.

My time with Butch turned out to be well spent. He was the first long-term friend of the Crazy Horse brothers I spent time with alone. I still had some questions about them, and I wanted to get Butch's assessment.

As we drove from one end of the reservation to the other, he recited the key points and histories of each community as we passed through them. He pointed out places important in Floyd, Doug, and Don's family histories. I took pictures all along the way, even though I was still having trouble with my camera's advance lever. He told me he found Floyd to be honest and truthful, but didn't know Doug and Don well enough to pass judgment.

I confided I was not one hundred percent sure they had accepted me, because they often declined to answer my questions. I surmised they might be keeping me at arm's length until they figured out what to do with me.

Butch just smiled. Then he told me a cautionary tale.

At one time Butch had been a member of a renowned Lakota drum group called the Bad Hands. He was with them when they went to Russia on a cultural exchange in the 1990s.

When their group arrived in Moscow, their tour bus motored by the crowds lining the streets to greet them. During their drive they spotted a man's head just behind the crowd that kept popping up and yelling, "Lakota." The man continued to follow their bus, bobbing up and down behind the crowd. So Butch and his drum group invited him to board their bus.

Once aboard, the Russian told them he was in a Russian drum group that sang Lakota songs. He asked if they had a tape of Lakota songs they could give him, so his drum group could learn them. The Bad Hands had brought no recordings with them, save one—a private recording one of their singers had made. It was the singer's only copy, and he didn't want to give it up. The rest of the Band Hand singers pressured him until he finally relented and gave it to the Russian.

Several months later, after Butch and his drum group had returned from Russia, a package arrived in the mail. Inside the package was a cassette tape from the Russian and his drum group with the songs they had learned from the Bad Hand singer's tape. The Bad Hands found their renditions horrendous. They turned to the member who had given up his precious tape and somberly informed him he had made a terrible mistake. They told him he had ruined Lakota music in the eyes of the world forever.

Then Butch burst into laughter as he tried to describe the look on this poor fellow's face. Once he caught his breath from laughing, he became deadly serious and said, "That is how you know you've been accepted. When they poke fun at you. It's our way."

Just prior to returning to Floyd's house, Butch pointed out a beautiful sunset directly in front of us and asked if I wanted to take a picture. I stopped the car to take a photo, but the advance lever stuck. As I tried to force it forward, I felt the film inside snap in two. I tried to fix it by putting the camera under my shirt. I opened it to reconnect the broken film to its spool. But my shirt slipped, and the film was exposed to the light—and ruined.

When we pulled back into Floyd's, he had finished tying the branches to form the skeleton frame of his new sweat lodge. Now he was building a fire so we could sweat. Since his new sweat had nothing to cover its frame yet, he was preparing the older, smaller sweat lodge for the ceremony.

"Got a great tour from Butch of the reservation," I informed Floyd.

"Did you get any pictures?" Floyd queried.

"I tried," I answered sheepishly.

Floyd smiled with a knowing look.

Later that night Floyd, Doug, Don, a few of their friends, and myself sweated. It was just as wonderful as the first time. I wanted to share this with members of my family. I asked if I could bring my nephews to the rez and sweat the next time we met.

"Why do you need to bring your nephews? Are you afraid to sweat alone with us?" Don asked accusingly.

Caught off guard, I didn't know how to respond.

That's when they burst out laughing. "Sure, bring them," Doug said with a smile.

They were poking fun at me, and I knew what it meant.

I couldn't wait to tell my nephews Michael and Geoffrey about their opportunity to sweat with the Crazy Horse Family. And when Karen heard I was taking my nephews to South Dakota for a sweat, she asked to come along.

That's when she made an extraordinary offer.

Apparently, my need for a video camera had not been forgotten. Knowing my credit was maxed out and that I had no savings, she offered to help me buy a professional video camera. She said she would put it on her credit card, but I would have to make the payments. I gratefully accepted. We shopped around and got a good camera, a JVC GY-DV500. It was huge by today's standards and lacking the high-definition function so prevalent today—but I loved it.

Her kindness became a pivotal event in my life.

At about the same time, the computer memory business no longer yielded the same profit margins it once did. My paychecks had shrunk. I didn't like my job—and doing it for peanuts made me like it even less. So I quit.

When my mom heard I had quit my job, she was elated. She invited me to stay with her. She had recently taken a nasty fall and was rehabbing at her home. She needed a caregiver. She couldn't think of anyone better to fill that role than her suddenly unemployed son. She offered me free rent and food. I needed both. So I accepted her request.

However, once August rolled around, I bid Mom adieu, and with Karen and my nephews in tow, I struck out for South Dakota by car.

After four days on the road, we arrived at Floyd's house. The first thing I did was show off my new video camera. It impressed them.

William Matson

However, my good news was tempered by some bad. Butch had passed away two days prior to our arrival. Although I barely knew him, I felt the loss. He had shared his knowledge, wisdom, and opinions with me unselfishly during our time together. His funeral was to be held the following evening.

I had suggested to my nephews and Karen that they give Floyd some tobacco and request a sweat with him and his brothers. After doing so, Floyd said he was okay with the nephews sweating, but he could not run a sweat with Karen. He had been told by his grandfathers he was to run sweats with only men. But he called in his cousin Morris to run a sweat for Karen and any other women who wanted to join in.

That night I sweated in the new Bear Lodge. Its bigger size caused the heat to rise and follow the contours of the dome ceiling to the lodge's outer edges, causing most of the heat to be felt on my back. Very different from the smaller sweat, where the heat came directly from the rocks into my chest and face. But it gave me the same positive, spiritual feeling. My nephews handled the sweat just fine. After the men finished, Karen and two women, entered the sweat lodge and sweated with Morris.

The following evening, I attended Butch's funeral with my nephews. The service was in a tribal community building. They sang the hymns in Lakota. It was a new experience for me to hear old standards like "Rock of Ages" and "Amazing Grace" in the Lakota language. But it was the way Butch would have wanted it, and that made me happy.

Afterwards, Floyd made a request. "Later this year we plan to go to Slim Buttes to find where our grandmother is laying. We were wondering if you could come and document it with your camera. It would be for the relatives that can't join us."

My heart smiled and my voice answered yes.

Then they told me about their grandmother.

They Are Afraid Of Her was the youngest sister of Crazy Horse's birth mother, Rattling Blanket Woman. She was a bit of a tomboy, with an independent spirit, and she helped teach young Crazy Horse to be self-reliant and hunt for game.

Earlier in her life she was known as Looks At It. She received her new name, They Are Afraid Of Her, when her husband tried to move her to a camp far away from her family. She loved her family and wanted to stay close to them. When he tried to force her to go, she turned on him and beat him up.

"How do you know all this?" I asked.

"One of our grandmothers told it to our grandfather, who passed it on to us," answered Doug.

"Which grandmother?" I asked.

"Iron Cedar, Crazy Horse's sister—and our grandmother." Doug answered.

My eyes nearly popped out of my head. "His sister? You told me he didn't have a sister."

"We wanted to see where the story went first before we told you," Doug replied.

They wanted to see where the story went first. The phrase hit me like a ton of bricks. They were testing me. Fortunately, I had kept their stories private, so I had at least passed their test. It made me wonder if there would be more tests down the road.

Later that evening, we planned our trip. We compared our individual schedules and agreed on the fall when we could all go to Slim Buttes and find They Are Afraid Of Her's grave together.

When the time came for our rendezvous, I flew out, rented a car, and drove directly to Floyd's, where I spent the night.

The next morning, we awoke to a few inches of snow on the ground.

In the Pacific Northwest I rarely saw snow, so the sight of it made me uneasy. I asked if we were still going.

Floyd, Doug, and Don laughed. "Of course we're still going," replied Don. "You're in South Dakota now. We see snow all the time. Besides, it's a wet snow. It'll be melted by the time we got to Slim Buttes."

I noticed Kevin was absent, so I asked about him.

"He can't make it, he's got woman problems," answered Doug.

I thought it strange that someone putting something as important as their oral history into book form would

Slim Buttes

not be there. But then again, maybe his woman problems were too severe.

By the time we got to Slim Buttes, the roads were clear and what remained of the snow was now slush. As we hiked into the pine trees and majestic buttes dominating the area, Floyd, Doug, and Don each went a separate direction. I followed Don.

Slim Buttes had a beauty and ruggedness to it I had never witnessed before. I asked Don how they knew where to find her grave. He told me the grandfathers and grandmothers had said to look for certain landmarks and those landmarks would lead them to her grave.

"What are the landmarks? Maybe I could help you look," I volunteered.

"The landmarks are for the family to find," he replied.

Slim Buttes area

Thus, for the rest of the afternoon, I wandered behind Don, waiting for him to find a landmark. It never happened.

On our drive back I mused, "I wish the snow would have stayed around, I could at least have had some cool snow shots."

"Be careful what you ask for. The Wakiyans might hear you and give you more than you can handle," Floyd warned.

A Wakiyan is a thunder being in the Lakota culture. They bring thunder, lightning, rain, wind, hail, snow, and everything weather related, including tornadoes.

"It still would have been cool to get some snow shots," I countered.

The brothers rolled their eyes and laughed.

Once home, Floyd announced they would make another try to find They Are Afraid Of Her's grave. "I think we probably just missed her," he declared.

"When do you want to try again?" I probed.

"When can you come back?" he asked.

I smiled. We decided an agreeable time would be just after Thanksgiving.

As I got ready to leave, Kevin showed up. We all took turns informing him how the day had gone.

Then as I left Floyd's house, he followed me to my car.

"It would be cool if we could exchange information on their stories," Kevin suggested.

"What information were you interested in?" I asked.

"Maybe you take some notes for me on your trips with them. In return I could tell you everything that I know."

"Why not go yourself, so you can see everything first hand?" I asked.

"I got some stuff I got to do," he answered.

"So you want me to write some notes for you?"

"Yeah, for the book. I could use the money."

It took all my concentration to make a decent documentary. Taking the time to take notes so he could "do other stuff" would only distract me. So I declined.

He nodded acknowledgement, and we parted ways.

Upon returning to Tacoma, Mom was still rehabbing. It wasn't going well. She had lost nearly all her confidence. I did all I could to help her believe in herself again. It took about a year. During that time, she rediscovered her ability to walk without a walker and to drive a car again. It made me feel good to see her back to being her old self.

Because of her re-found confidence, she insisted on being the head cook for our Thanksgiving dinner that year.

Thanksgiving at Mom's house required a full day of cooking food. Mom always made too much and then encouraged us to overeat. We would protest—and then eventually take another helping. It was a tradition. Then after our feast we would all huddle around the television and fall sleep.

Once the Thanksgiving weekend was over, I packed and prepared for my return to South Dakota.

Upon landing in Rapid City, light snow flurries greeted me, light enough that I didn't worry. I rented a car and took off for Floyd's. Snow started coming down heavier. Eventually the wind picked up, and the snow started blowing across the road, similar to sand in a sandstorm. In South Dakota, they call it a ground blizzard.

When I spotted buffalo at a ranch near the road during my drive, I stopped to film them. They trudged, head first, into the windblown snow. It would be great footage for my proposed documentary on Crazy Horse. Back into my warm car, I dreamed about the possibilities of all the great shots I could get with snow. As I continued my drive, the windswept snow increased in density until it became a full-fledged blizzard.

About ten miles from Floyd's house, I lost control of the car on a slick spot and plowed into a snowbank bordering the road. When I tried to back out, I found I was stuck. Several concerned motorists stopped to see if they could help. I told them to please call a tow truck. Each person said they would.

I waited. Two hours passed. I continued to stay in my car and wonder why the tow truck was taking so long. As day turned to dusk, no tow truck came. I became concerned. I had left my car motor running the entire time to keep warm, but I didn't want to spend the night in the car.

The end of November can be mighty cold in South Dakota. It is normally twenty to forty degrees colder than the Pacific Northwest during the winter months.

Finally, a police car pulled up and asked if I needed some help.

"I'm waiting for a tow. I've been waiting about two hours now."

"They don't run in this kind of weather. Could I take you somewhere?" the policeman replied.

"Really? Tow trucks don't run in the snow here?" I asked in disbelief. It was hard for me to fathom. Seemed like a snowstorm would provide a lot of business.

"No. I'm the only help you will get. Can I take you somewhere?" he repeated.

I told the policeman he could take me to Floyd's house. So he did.

When Floyd learned about my plight, he scolded me. "You wished for the snow, so the Wakiyans gave it you."

I wasn't sure how connected my wishing for snow and the actual snow storm were, but I accepted his premise.

Floyd then called Don, who had a four-wheel-drive truck, to come and lend a hand.

Once Don arrived, we all climbed into his truck and went to retrieve my car.

After reaching my car, Don got out, got down on his hands and knees, and examined the situation. I watched him uncover my rear tires with a small shovel and later with his hands to clear a path for my car to back out. He suggested I get in my car and start it up, to stay warm.

After climbing in and starting it, I waited for about ten minutes and became bored. I wanted to be more involved. So I got out to ask what I could do to help. Unfortunately, I had left the car running—*and in gear.* The snow bank had kept the car from moving, causing me to believe the car was in park. When I closed the door, I heard the car doors automatically lock.

My heart sank.

As Don continued to dig the rear end of my car out, I didn't know quite how to tell him what I had done. So I hopped inside his warm truck where I found Doug and Floyd.

Finally, Don returned to his truck and peaked in at me. "I need you to get in your car and steer. I'll pull you out with a chain," he said matter-of-factly.

I felt small. I had to tell him what I didn't want to tell him.

"I don't know how you're going to take this, but I locked myself out of the car."

There was a very long, uncomfortable silence.

Once my words sank in, Don repeated them, "You locked yourself out of your car?"

"Yeah," I answered. My face was red as a beet.

"Well, I can't pull you out without someone steering," he said exasperated.

I felt a foreboding guilt descend upon me.

"There's a ranch house just up the road. Maybe they have a coat hanger we can use," Floyd offered.

So we drove about three hundred yards to the ranch house.

Floyd and Don told me to stay in the truck while they went to talk to the rancher. I couldn't blame them. I had already caused enough trouble. After talking to the rancher, they came back and told me he would get his tractor.

"A tractor? What for?" I asked.

"To pull you out," Floyd stated, with a hint of disgust.

At that point I figured it was best not to speak.

We headed back to my car and waited for the tractor. As it came into view, it had great big monster truck rear wheels. The tractor lumbered over to my car, where Don had hooked a chain to the car's rear undercarriage. The rancher pulled it out of the snow with little effort. He then towed it down the street towards his place. He had to keep his speed up to keep the car from sliding back into the ditch along the icy road. He towed it into his barn and shut the doors behind it.

We followed, and Don pulled up next to the garage and said, "I hear this guy's barn used to be a chop shop."

Alarmed, I quickly found my way into the barn.

No chop shop. They had been joking—again.

Instead I saw a ranch hand forcing a crowbar over the top of the driver's door to create enough room to get a coat hanger inside the car. My heart sank as I saw the car door bend outward in an ugly fashion, making a crease in the upper window frame of the door. I had not purchased rental car insurance.

Finally, they worked the hanger around the inside door handle and opened it. However, the paint where the crowbar was used to jimmy the door open was gone. A fresh paint job would be necessary to restore it back to its original state. I began calculating what the cost of a fresh paint job would be. Bottom line was I wasn't sure I had enough money or credit to cover it.

Floyd woke me from my calculations, "Let me drive it to the house."

I couldn't say no. We thanked the rancher and his crew and took off.

The next morning Floyd, Doug, Don, and myself went to Slim Buttes. In Don's truck. Slim Buttes had a fresh covering of snow, giving it a fresh beauty. The pine trees reminded me of the white flocked trees that I had seen as a kid in the expensive section of a Christmas tree lot. We looked all day for They Are Afraid Of Her's grave. Again, we ended finding nothing. But I got some great snow shots.

"I guess she doesn't want to be found yet," Floyd speculated on the ride home.

That night we had a superb sweat.

After our sweat, we sat down to eat. During the meal, Floyd told me they had been invited to a meeting at the

Little Bighorn Battlefield National Monument in early spring. The National Park Service had asked them to offer input on an Indian Memorial that was to be built there.

"Bring your camera," Floyd said, "in case the park service tries to pull a fast one. This way we'll have it all on video."

His request came as a relief—they had forgiven me for the trouble I had caused.

I agreed.

The next morning I prepared to drive to the airport. Knowing I was worried about the ugly scrape on the inside lip of the door, Floyd suggested I get a sharpie of the same color (light blue) and color it in so it wouldn't be so noticeable. I did. It didn't hide it at all. It made the scrape stand out even more.

So I drove to the airport, ready to accept my fate, when it began snowing again. In fact, it snowed so hard that inspecting the inside of the rental car in their outdoor lot would not be pleasant. I thought just maybe the Creator was smiling on me that day. The people at the rental car place never checked the car.

Chapter Seven

The Little Bighorn Battlefield

F OR DECADES, THE LAKOTA and Cheyenne kept silent about their losses at the Battle of the Little Bighorn. Fear of government reprisals fueled their desire for anonymity. As a result, historians for over one hundred years have stated the Lakota and Cheyenne casualties at the battle were light or nearly non-existent.

Now it was time for truth—not only for their own people but for the world to know the sacrifices made by their grandfathers.

Sitting Bull, Crazy Horse, and the Lakota, Dakota, Nakota, Cheyenne, and Arapaho Nations had delivered a message to the American government that the ground they hunted on and called home was not for the government to take. On June 25, 1876, the government sent an arrogant cavalry commander, Lieutenant Colonel George Armstrong Custer, and his 7th Cavalry, to attack their peaceful village. To attack their homes. To attack their families. To force their nations to submit and abandon their way of life and the lands they lived on.

However, the Lakota and their allies believed too deeply in the sanctity of Mother Earth and their way of life to roll over. And Custer and his men paid the ultimate price for attempting to carry out the government's will.

Many from the Native nations died that day, as well. To those nations, the Little Bighorn National Battlefield is sacred ground.

Following the battle, Lakota, Dakota, Nakota, and Cheyenne families placed smooth river rocks as markers on the battlefield to remember where family members had fallen. So in reality, they had already started an Indian Memorial.

The Little Bighorn Battlefield National Monument grounds cover 1.196 miles and are visited by around half a million visitors every year. It wasn't always the Little Bighorn Battlefield National Monument, though. At one time it was the Custer Battlefield National Monument. On December 10, 1991, Public Law 102-201 was passed by Congress and signed by President George H. W. Bush, authorizing the name change. It proclaimed the Custer Battlefield National Monument would forever after be known as the Little Bighorn Battlefield National Monument. The same bill also authorized an Indian Memorial to be constructed to honor the Natives who fought there.

The name change was not welcomed by all. Some believed the National Monument should be there to honor only those who died fighting with Custer.

Barbara Booher (now Barbara Sutteer), a Native, was named the battlefield's Park Superintendent during the time of the name change. Her heritage made her an easy

Custer Battlefield postcard published prior to the name change

target for those who detested the change. I had the privilege to talk with her and other past park superintendents in 2003. I learned that she had received death threats during her time as superintendent. Specifically, for being the person in charge. However, she persevered and won accolades among her peers for demonstrating the courage to stand her ground.

In late 1993 Gerard Baker, another Native, replaced Booher as Park Superintendent. The choice of another Native disheartened those who opposed the memorial. They greeted Baker, like Booher before him, with racism, threats, and insults. He, too, persevered.

Finally in 1996, when it came time for the government to become serious about building the Indian Memorial, they started their quest by calling for submissions of the memorial's design theme.

After reviewing all the submissions, the government selected a winning theme, based on a quote from the Lakota elder Enos Poor Bear Sr.: "Peace through Unity." The phrase spoke to both the Native and American sides to put aside their differences for the common good. Many felt the selection fitting, as Poor Bear Sr. and a Northern Cheyenne, Austin Two Moons, had been two of the principal proponents pushing the park service for an Indian Memorial for years.

Another who pushed for a memorial, according to park rangers, was the activist Russell Means. In 1972, Means and a group of like-minded advocates came to the battlefield to install a cast-iron memorial plaque of their own to honor the fallen Natives. The Park Superintendent during that time, Eldon Reyer, talked them out of installing it by promising to initiate a proper monument through the park service.

Means and the others believed Reyer. They waited fifteen years for the park service to fulfill Reyer's promise.

Nothing ever happened.

Finally in 1987, Means and two activists, Chauncey Whitwright III and Tim Lame Woman, concluded they would no longer wait for the park service to fulfill what was obviously an empty promise. They would install a plaque of their own and vowed to make their installation permanent.

To prepare for this, Lame Woman engaged George Magpie, a welder by trade and a member of the Northern Cheyenne Reservation, to make the plaque. Lame Woman had him engrave an inscription on it, reading: "In honor of our Indian patriots who fought and defeated the U.S. Cavalry to save our women and children from mass murder. In doing so, preserving our rights to our homelands, treaties, and sovereignty."

With plaque in hand, they set their plan in motion to coincide with the 112th anniversary of the battle, in 1988.

On the morning of June 25, Means, Hank Adams, Whitwright, Lame Woman, and Two Moons, among others, drove to the Little Bighorn battlefield and made their way up Last Stand Hill to the memorial commemorating Custer's men. They peeled a swath of sod out of the lawn next to the soldier's monument. Then they poured cement into the opening and placed their plaque into the wet cement.

Once installed, they warned the park service that if the plaque was removed, then they would remove the one for Custer and his men. The Park Superintendent at the time was Dennis Ditmanson. He promised not to remove their plaque and told them he would work to gain approval for a formal monument.

The park service kept its word this time. The approval came via the legislation passed in 1991. The activists were cautiously pleased.

Again, not everyone was happy.

Opposition formed from those believing the National Monument should only honor the soldiers.

Fortunately, the desire of the park service to build the Indian Memorial continued to push ahead. Unfortunately, the government's efforts to build a proper memorial were clumsy. The government awarded the physical design of the memorial to a non-Native. A non-Native who knew little about the Native cultures involved in the battle.

Against this background, Floyd, Doug, Don, myself, and their cousins, Scott Dupris and Carl Dupree, arrived at a meeting hosted by the park service to elicit input on the memorial design from the Native tribes who took part in the battle. I was the only non-Native other than a few park rangers to attend the meeting. Filming was not allowed.

The meeting began with a Native prayer. Following the prayer, the rangers passed out large envelopes filled with the government's proposal for the memorial's construction, along with a mock-up drawing. The mock-up showed a circular stone wall with the outer portion of the wall nearly covered by a berm of dirt. On the north side, the wall was open except for three, wiry iron sculptures of warriors on horseback and a Native woman bringing a shield to the lead rider. Entrance into the memorial's interior occurred with two narrow breaks in the wall, from the east and west. Long poles that extended several feet into the sky, with flags atop, flanked either side of the eastern entrance. The inner walls of the circle were populated with panels that would contain messages and images yet to be determined.

After everybody made a quick study of the design, Carl spoke first.

"These poles with the flags at the top have no connection to any of our plains tribes. They aren't part of our culture. They look more like goal posts from an NFL football game."

His comment elicited several snickers, which kicked off roughly an hour of trashing the pole portion of the design.

Soon the criticisms extended to the entire design, and the Natives who had fought so long to have a memorial built worried. They feared the outrage over the poles would be so great that the memorial might end up being abandoned altogether. So they began to defend it. At that point, arguing and insults filled the air, lasting until lunch time.

Finally, with full bellies and cooler heads prevailing in the afternoon, they decided to eliminate the poles. The circular design would remain. With that, they adjourned the meeting, though everyone agreed another meeting was needed at a later date. Meanwhile, the design could be taken back to the respective reservations for additional evaluations from those who had not attended the meeting.

Before we left, newly appointed Superintendent Darrell J. Cook approached Floyd, Doug, and Don, asking them to stay an additional day. He and some other rangers wanted to talk to them about Crazy Horse and learn what they might know about the battle. Cook offered lodging for the night in the neighboring town of Hardin. Since I was Floyd, Doug, and Don's ride home, he also asked me to stay.

The next morning, we met with Cook and the battlefield's museum curator, Kitty Deernose. They took us to a vault underneath the Visitor's Center where they kept the artifacts collected over time that pertained to the battle. We saw one of Custer's guidons enclosed under glass. It looked fragile and ready to fall apart if they ever removed it from its enclosure. We also saw a variety of bullets, shells, arrowheads, and other artifacts retrieved from the battlefield.

After observing the artifacts, the rangers sat us down to learn what Floyd, Doug, and Don knew about the battle and Crazy Horse's participation in it. Park Historian John Doerner took notes. They gave the rangers their description of the fight and where some of the participants had fallen, helping clear some gray areas the rangers had been struggling with.

Once they fed us, we headed back to the Cheyenne River Rez. On the way Floyd, Doug, and Don mused about riding horses to the Little Bighorn Indian Memorial, in remembrance of the warriors who had fought there. A three-hundred-sixty-mile ride. They figured they could camp along the highway at night. During our drive back, I saw few campgrounds on the route they were talking about taking. I wondered if a ride was even possible, with all the cars and trucks whizzing past and possibly spooking the horses. But I stayed mum.

After a while their musings expanded into adding a ride to Crazy Horse Mountain, after the Little Bighorn ride, to help the sculptor Ziolkowski's widow, Ruth, celebrate her birthday on June 26. Ruth was currently overseeing the carving of Crazy Horse.

"We should call Donnie Sprague and let him know," Floyd said.

"Who's Donnie Sprague?" I asked.

"Donovin Sprague. He's a relative that works at the Mountain," Floyd replied.

"At the gift shop?"

"No, he works at the cultural center there," came the answer.

I was not aware the Mountain had a culture center. They explained that Donovin had been acquiring copies of pictures of their relatives from some Lakota who visited the Mountain. They informed me he was a descendant of Hump, Crazy Horse's uncle.

I asked if it would be all right to visit him. They said yes. So, once I dropped them off, I drove to Crazy Horse Mountain hoping to get to know Donovin.

I found him in the aforementioned Crazy Horse Mountain Cultural Center building, a place where the Natives displayed and sold their crafts and artwork to tourists. He was knowledgeable and had a lot of formal book learning. He showed me several pictures Lakota families had given to him at the Mountain. He also had a handle on their genealogy.

I saw him as a resource I could turn to if I didn't understand an aspect of their family tree or needed a family photo. After bidding him adieu, I spent the next two days driving back to my mother's place. Once there, I waited for Floyd, Doug, and Don to call, asking for a ride to their next meeting at the Little Bighorn.

That call came in the early spring.

During my drive to the rez, the Little Bighorn Battlefield's Kitty Deernose called to ask if I knew who the closest living relative to Sitting Bull was. It perplexed me why she would think I knew. I was a friend to a handful in the Clown family, but not to the entire Lakota nation.

She said, "I've heard a man named Ron McNeil, from the Standing Rock Reservation, is the closest living relative to Sitting Bull, but I'm not sure. I want to invite Sitting Bull's closest relative to the unveiling of the Indian Memorial."

I was just learning about the Lakota myself. However, having met Donovin, I thought it would be an excellent test of his knowledge. I promised to get back to her with what I learned.

Donovin informed me that a Lakota, Ernie LaPointe, and his sisters Ethel, Lydia, and Darlene were Sitting Bull's closest living relatives. I reported this news back to Deernose. She thanked me and said she would get in touch with them.

Upon arriving at the Cheyenne River Rez, I picked up Floyd, Doug, and Don, and we motored out to attend my second meeting at the Little Bighorn Battlefield National Monument.

A representative of the Pine Ridge Reservation, Vice Chairman Dennis King, was there. He opened the meeting by announcing that his reservation was introducing an injunction to stop the construction of the Indian Memorial.

King contended he and his rez were not happy with one of the wiry metal warrior sculptures. Specifically, the warrior being handed a shield by a woman. King claimed women did not help Lakota warriors get dressed for battle. The sculpture misrepresented his people. He claimed the park service was romanticizing the battle at the expense of the Lakota people. After stating his position, he passed out copies of the proposed injunction to all the attendees.

Once all had read it, it was met with an explosion of angry voices. Whitwright was the loudest. He slammed down King's injunction and pounded his fist into the table so hard it seemed the table would break.

"This means war!" he shouted angrily at King. It was the first time I had ever heard that phrase used outside of a Hollywood movie.

The scene became surreal as Whitwright brought a veracity to his argument that became contagious. Arguing and outright hostility blossomed between King and the supporters of the memorial. Nobody heard anybody. It felt like a fistfight would break out any minute. The park rangers were at a loss on how to calm this storm of anger.

Then a Native named Linus End of Horn, who claimed to be a descendant of the Lakota warrior Gall, stood up and asked to speak.

His voice was calm. His demeanor mesmerizing. His delivery eloquent.

"The cottonwood is our most sacred tree," he said with a reverence in his voice. "It is the tree of our Sundance. Let me tell you something told to me by my grandparents on how our families and all our people are sacred.

"Our men are like the cottonwood trunk and its main branches. Strong. Keeps the tree upright, just like the tipi poles that hold up our tipis. Our women are like cottonwood leaves that give shelter and comfort from the heavy rain, snow, hailstorms, and hot sun. Leaves that curl and wrap around our tipi poles to keep in the warmth and give our men a place to find cover from the Wakiyans. And the cottonwood roots, like the tipi pegs, are the children that hold our families in place. It would not be a cottonwood without the trunk, branches, leaves, and roots. It would not be a tipi without the tipi poles, outside covering, and pegs. We would not be a family without a man, a woman, and children. Without our families, our nation would not exist. If the memorial is to represent our nation, let it represent our entire nation. Let our women be represented."

The room went silent.

The woman handing the shield to the warrior at the Indian Memorial stayed—along with the rest of the memorial. The ugly acrimony transformed into a happy ending. The memorial now would be a reality.

After the meeting Floyd, Doug, Don, Carl, and Scott discussed the feasibility of riding their horses through the battlefield to honor their ancestors with the park rangers.

Indian Memorial wire figures
Photo by Mark Frethem

After much deliberation, the rangers granted them permission to ride over the battlefield. It also meant riding to the battlefield on horseback was no longer just an idea. It was real.

Then the rangers asked Floyd if he would do them a favor and write a few words on behalf of the Crazy Horse family that they could inscribe onto a panel inside the memorial. Floyd agreed.

After returning to the rez, I stayed a few extra days. During this time, I got my courage up and proposed doing a documentary on Crazy Horse based on the family's oral history, passed to Floyd, Doug, and Don. They mulled it over. Finally, Doug approached me and asked if I would like to come on the ride to the Little Bighorn and take a few video shots of their journey.

Although it wasn't what I had proposed, I agreed.

"I'll even shoot some of the ride while riding horseback."

My pledge to video while on horseback made them laugh. They told me filming while I was riding would never happen—at least not with *me* in the saddle.

I tucked their needling away in my memory and promised myself I would have the last laugh.

Chapter Eight
The Ride

A FTER SPENDING TIME AT my mom's, I returned to the rez. I found preparations for the horseback ride in full swing. Floyd, Doug, Don, Scott, and Carl were all making it happen. They were calling it the "Great Sioux Nation Victory Ride." The Great Sioux Nation is a term the world uses to describe when the Lakota, Dakota, and Nakota Tribes are unified as one.

With all the excitement surrounding the ride, I wasn't content with taking a few random video shots as they requested. I wanted to do more. I decided to make a feature-length documentary.

They informed me the Cheyenne River tribal government was donating a buffalo to the ride. However, it still needed to be killed. Tribal officials planned to kill it during a hunt. I requested and was given permission to film it.

When Floyd, Don, and myself arrived for the hunt, we found a single buffalo in an acre of fenced pasture. The tribe's plan was to drive a Ford Ranger truck into the pasture and shoot the buffalo from the truck's driver's seat. I had expected the hunt to actually be a hunt. However, nothing ventured, nothing gained, so I decided to film it, anyway. To get an unencumbered view with my camera, I elected to position myself inside the truck's bed.

As we entered the pasture where the buffalo was grazing, our truck stopped twenty yards away from it. The driver grabbed a rifle from his companion in the passenger seat and took careful aim. Fired. The buffalo flinched but did not fall. It just kept eating grass. The driver shot again. The buffalo flinched again, but stood. A third shot rang out, and the buffalo stopped grazing and stared at us.

The buffalo's stare unnerved the driver, causing him to back up the truck in great haste. His maneuver caught me by surprise. I lost my balance and fell on my backside in the truck bed.

After the truck stopped and I recovered from my fall, I found the buffalo once again nonchalantly grazing, as though nothing had happened.

The driver repositioned the truck. I lined up the buffalo in my camera viewfinder. Crack! Another shot shattered the air. This time the buffalo was clearly annoyed and its tail went straight up. When a buffalo's tail stands straight up, and it's not relieving itself, it means it is angry and likely to charge.

Again the truck went into reverse, and again I was jolted to my backside. I now realized filming from the bed of a truck while playing cat and mouse with an angry buffalo was a mistake. I knew if the buffalo successfully charged, it was big enough to knock our truck over. It was also strong enough that if it threw me from the truck, it could easily gore me to death—providing the driver's unpredictable maneuvers didn't kill me first.

When the truck stopped again, the buffalo turned toward us as if to charge. Seeing this, the driver drove the truck forward to confuse it. He then stopped and fired two quick shots. The buffalo fell.

"Yes!" the driver yelled. His celebration was short lived.

The buffalo got back up with its tail raised stiffly. The truck zipped with extraordinary speed backwards, and I slid around in the truck bed like a silver ball in a pinball machine.

I felt the bruises multiplying all over my body, but I kept my camera from hitting the truck bed wall. How I managed that, I really don't know.

Once again, the driver inched closer and fired. The buffalo did not fall. He fired again. The buffalo stayed upright. It seemed this buffalo was immortal.

The rifle cracked again and the buffalo finally fell again.

We waited.

After determining the buffalo was not getting back up, the driver drove over to it and cautiously poked it with his rifle barrel from the window of the truck's cab. The buffalo did not respond.

The driver got out and offered tobacco to the four cardinal directions, and then down to the earth and up to the sky. He prayed. Then sprinkled the tobacco on the buffalo as an offering of thanks for the buffalo sacrificing its life to feed the people.

As a last act, he took his knife and cut the buffalo's throat to ensure it stayed dead. After the buffalo had bled a sufficient amount, Floyd, Don, and the others came out and picked up the huge buffalo, weighing about a ton, and loaded it in the truck bed. We walked behind the truck as they drove it out of the pasture.

Once out of the pasture, they lifted it onto a hoist by tying a rope around its rear legs and hanging the rope onto a hook attached to the hoist. They pulled it up and while it hung free, they skinned it.

The tribal government kept the hide because it was worth significant money. We kept the carcass of meat and loaded it in the back of Don's truck.

On the drive back, Floyd said, "Their rifle was too light a caliber. I don't like seeing a buffalo suffer. A bigger caliber rifle could have ended his life quicker and kept it from suffering."

Floyd, Doug, and Don's other brother, Blaine Clown Jr., whom I barely knew because he kept to himself, butchered the carcass into stew meat for the riders to eat during their ride.

During a break from preparations, I asked Floyd if anybody from the Pine Ridge, Rosebud, or Standing Rock reservations would join us. He took that opportunity to tell me those from Pine Ridge, who called themselves Oglala and those from Rosebud, who called themselves Sicangu, had their lineage wrong. He said the Oglala and Sicangu were not Lakota bands.

The Pine Ridge Rez had always been referred to as the home of the Oglala, while the Rosebud Rez was home to the Sicangu band. The Hunkpapa band inhabited the Standing Rock Rez. The Minikouju, Itazipco, Sihasapa, and Owehenupa bands made up the Cheyenne River Rez.

Virtually every book I read on the Lakota said they were comprised of seven bands. The books all agreed the seven were the Minikouju, Hunkpapa, Itazipco, Sihasapa, Owehenupa, Sicangu, and Oglala. But Floyd said that was not true.

"Then what are the Oglala and Sicangu?" I asked.

He told me they were bands formed by the government.

"Does that mean there are only five bands?"

"There are seven."

"Then who are the other two?"

"Cuthead," he answered.

Books that I had read said the Cutheads were a "sub-band." But what is a sub-band? And who makes the judgment to call them a sub-band? And did the Cutheads agree they were a sub-band? That was unlikely, since the concept of a sub-band seemed to be born from the American and European need for order. The Cutheads were also signatory to the Fort Laramie Treaty of 1868. I concluded it was plausible the Cuthead were a band.

"And who is the other one?"

Floyd thought for a moment and said, "Flathead."

"Flathead?" I asked in surprise.

The Flathead are a tribe in northwestern Montana. They spoke a different language. Privately I wondered if this came from their oral history or if he just had a bone to pick with the Oglala and Sincagu bands. But Butch had vouched for Floyd's honesty. I wanted a reason to buy in.

So I challenged him and asked why the Flathead spoke Salish, a substantially different language than Lakota.

"I have spoken the truth," said Floyd. The tone of his answer told me not to ask about it any further. For years I pondered this revelation, believing at some point I would find the resolution I was looking for.

Finally, the time came to ride.

The family cemetery was designated as the starting point, situated three miles east of the community of Thunder Butte. The cemetery was comprised of aging metal, wooden, and concrete grave markers designating where their deceased family members were buried. A wire mesh fence with a swinging metal gate enclosed the property, which had been the original homesite of Julia and Amos Clown who, in the Lakota way of life, were the biological grandparents of Floyd, Doug, and Don.

The riders planned to follow the same route their grandfathers took to the Little Bighorn in 1876. Carl and Scott would select where we would spend our nights.

Twenty-seven horses and over thirty riders were ready on June 9th for the first day of the ride. The morning was overcast. My camera was ready. More riders would join us once we neared to the battlefield.

Our ride had to reach the battlefield in time to make the memorial's dedication on the 127th anniversary of the battle, June 25, 2003. But since this was the first time they had attempted this ride, whether they arrived on time was an open question. However, they believed they would, with time to spare. To keep the horses and riders fresh to maintain their schedule, they decided to change both horses and riders every ten miles.

As they saddled up, Floyd approached each horse and marked its forehead with red earth paint. Then he prayed for the horse to have a safe journey. Finally, he smudged it with a twist of burning sweetgrass. Smudging is a form of purifying. He did it by covering the horse with a layer of smoke generated from the burning twist, as a blessing to ensure they finished the journey in good health.

Monte Condon, a Lakota singer, sang a Lakota prayer for their safe journey while accompanying himself on a hand drum as the ride began. Everything about the send-off felt good. I got some great shots of them riding away. Optimism ruled—until a powerful thunderstorm struck. The rain came down so heavily we lost all sight and contact with them.

As night fell, an uneasiness filled our campsite on Rabbit Creek, about thirty-two miles north of Maurine, SD. Nobody had heard from the riders. The half-moon that could have partially lit their way to our camp was blocked by a heavy cloud covering.

Worry set in. Vehicles took off to look for them.

Finally, to the relief of all, they arrived in camp, tired and hungry but in high spirits. Once in camp, the riders' first order of business was to water, unsaddle, groom, and feed their horses.

The cooks had kept the food simmering in anticipation of their arrival. And sure enough, the riders brought their appetites. They lined up to fill their paper plates with baked beans and coleslaw. They dished buffalo stew into styrofoam bowls and ate with plastic flatware while sitting around our campfires, telling stories about their harrowing ride through the storm.

That night everybody slept good, and all was well.

However, the next morning the owner of the land we camped on woke us and demanded to know why we were camping on her land. Apparently, nobody had checked with her or asked for permission. This revelation caught most of us by surprise. We packed up as rapidly as we could.

Many of the adult riders who had not ridden in a long time were now sore beyond belief, and getting off her land in a hurry made them look like they were part of a fire drill at an old folks' home.

During the night, additional horses and riders had arrived. However, these fresh horses did not get marked or smudged in the rush to vacate the campsite.

Once clear of the campsite, we huddled around Carl and his laptop computer. It showed a map of our route to the Little Bighorn. Seeing it on a computer screen somehow made our future campsites seem more assured.

Scott and Carl drove ahead to secure our next campsite. As evening approached, they returned and directed our riders to a spot next to a small pond. However, as we rode into the campsite, a rancher pulled up in his pickup and told us it was his land and we did not have permission to camp.

Again, we left in a hurry, without knowing where we were going.

As the sun set, we still had no word on where we were to camp. Anxiety set in. Sensing this, Scott and Carl pointed to a field they said was BLM (Bureau of Land Management) land and open to the public.

It was a wheat field nearly ready for harvest.

I immediately had my doubts. I turned to Floyd, "I don't think this land is BLM land. And if it is, whoever planted the wheat will not like us setting up our tents on it."

Floyd agreed and confronted Scott and Carl. He asked how they knew it was BLM land. The answer to his question was silence. That told us all we needed to know. Gloom and doom replaced anxiety. Without a campsite, we'd have to turn around and go home.

At this point, I decided to get involved. I suggested we ask a rancher for permission to camp.

"We can't just knock on these white people's doors. They'll hurt us or have us thrown in jail," came the retort.

I understood their reluctance, predicated on their past dealings with white people outside the rez. Prejudice was more than just a word to them. All of them had been victims of bigotry their entire lives.

However, I was white, so maybe these white ranchers would listen to me. I proposed to do the knocking.

"What's the worst thing that could happen?" I asked. "That they say no?"

With that attitude, I approached the nearest ranch house and knocked. The house belonged to the Wayne Besler family. Nobody answered. So I walked out to their barn and called to see if anyone answered. They appeared.

I explained I was traveling with the Crazy Horse family and other Lakota riders to the Little Bighorn. I asked if they would grant us permission to spend the night in one of their fields.

"Of course," they answered.

They gave us a corral for our horses and bales of hay to feed them. The field they offered had fresh, running creek water for the horses. They treated us like royalty. Bigotry didn't seem to be a word the Besler's had in their vocabulary. In exchange, they asked if a Crazy Horse family member would tell them about some tipi rings on their land. Floyd, Doug, and Don agreed without hesitation.

A tipi ring is a ring of rocks placed at the base of the tipi wall to anchor its covering and seal the inside of the tipi from the outside cold. When the tipi's occupants moved camp, the rings remained.

The next morning Floyd, Doug, Don, myself, and two members of the Besler family drove to a place called Rabbit Butte. There we found three tipi rings. After examining them, Floyd, Doug, and Don said it looked like a scout camp set up as a lookout for a larger village.

We then climbed to the top of Rabbit Butte, which was the nearest butte in relation to the tipi rings. There we could see for miles.

Doug informed the Beslers and myself that with the aid of a mirror and the sun, a scout could signal larger villages of advancing danger or an approaching buffalo herd. The Besler's were grateful for the information, and we thanked them again for the help. Then we headed back to camp.

Upon our return, we found the riders mounted in a circle praying. It would be something they would repeat every morning during the ride. After they finished their prayer, they rode single file in a circle to get focused. Once focused they rode onto the road and started the day's ride.

However, one of the newly arrived horses that didn't get smudged had become ill. They had no choice but to leave it behind. A rider named Darwin Fast Horse stayed behind to look after him.

I asked if they wanted me to drive ahead and find our next campsite. Scott and Carl told me they had already chosen one, Slim Buttes. But I was welcome to find the next campsite after that.

"Here all this time we thought Bill was traveling with us," Carl said with a smile. "But after last night, now we're traveling with Bill." Everyone laughed and I felt their trust.

Then Floyd hopped into my car and said, "Let's go check out Slim Buttes."

Great Sioux Nation Victory Ride—a 360-mile horseback ride
Photo by Mark Frethem

And just like that, Floyd and I were on our way to Slim Buttes.

We played a tape of Lakota songs full blast with the car windows down on my tape player as we drove. I may not have been a Lakota, but I sure felt the Lakota spirit on our drive. Later, we found our campsite in the Slim Buttes National Forest.

Floyd told me Slim Buttes was sacred to his family. Besides harboring the elusive grave of They Are Afraid Of Her, another of their relatives, Bear With Horns, who died from wounds received at the Battle of the Little Bighorn, was buried there. Because of its importance to the family, they planned to spend two nights there.

Once we arrived at Slim Buttes, several of our riders wanted to clean themselves. None of us had showered since we left the rez. Floyd, Don, Scott, and I drove to the nearest town—Buffalo, South Dakota. Someone told them we could use the showers in the Buffalo High School gym. However, we found the building locked for the summer. Next we tried a local convenience store that advertised showers. The clerk there told us their shower was out of order.

Now desperate, we drove around Buffalo looking for a motel as a last resort. There was only one. I went inside to book a room so we could take showers. A middle-aged woman greeted me.

"We'd like a room," I announced.

"For how many?" she asked.

"Not sure. Maybe twenty to thirty. We're on a ride to the Little Bighorn and we're starting to become a little ripe," I answered, trying to inject a little humor into my request.

"What ride?" she queried.

"The Crazy Horse family and riders from the Great Sioux Nation Victory Ride," I responded.

"We got nothing available," she said coldly.

I couldn't believe it. There were only two cars in her lot, and I counted at least fourteen units at the site.

I asked her if she was so full then where were all the people.

"They're arriving later tonight," she retorted.

"What time?" I pressed.

"Late," she said, beginning to show her irritation over my questioning.

"Well, how about if we shower now and pay you for a full night? We promise to be out of here before the sun goes down," I propositioned.

"I don't know, if there's a lot of you, you might scare some of my other occupants."

"Why would your occupants be frightened of us?" I asked.

"Not you, your friends," she replied.

"Oh, I see, the Lakota," I said with a hint of disgust. "Well, if I promise you we will leave before nightfall, will you let us shower?"

"Not nightfall. Five p.m.," she countered.

I took a quick look at my watch.

"That's only three hours," I objected.

"Take it or leave it," she stated.

I paid for a full night. We brought in the riders to shower in shifts. We barely met our 5 p.m. checkout time. The entire episode was an eye opener. Not everyone was like the Beslers.

While we camped at Slim Buttes, they showed me a Crazy Horse family campsite, centuries old. Tall buttes on three sides, like a box canyon, shielded it from the northern, western, and southern winds. From the top of its towering buttes, you could see all the way to Rabbit Butte. I asked if this was one of the villages the scouts at Rabbit Butte communicated with. "Could be," Doug answered.

Our stay at Slim Buttes was an adventure in beauty and tranquility. However, during our last day there, a South Dakota state official approached us and said the water from the spring that supplied our campsite spigot had become contaminated because of the waste material generated from a nearby uranium mining site. He was there to shut the water off.

It was a reminder of how poorly those who had invaded the Lakota homelands had taken care of Mother Earth in the name of greed. We left immediately.

Once again, Floyd and I drove ahead to find our next campsite. We stopped at Camp Crook, South Dakota, a town of sixty-five people, on the Little Missouri River. There we found a National Forest Service Ranger named Jerry Martinez willing to put us up on his little ranch.

Camp Crook is off the beaten path. It was a two-and-one-half hour drive to the nearest supermarket, with fifty-five miles of that drive on a gravel road. Prior to becoming Camp Crook, it was the home to a Lakota campsite and gateway to the Sheep Mountains. The Sheep Mountains are beautiful and seemingly untouched by modern civilization—one of the most pristine areas I ever visited.

Prior to the ride, the family told me that during the Lakota tribe's free-roaming days, a warrior could ride over a hundred miles a day. More, if they traveled at night. At first, I had a hard time believing that. But after becoming a part of the ride, I became a believer. Our riders averaged around thirty miles per day. Occasionally they exceeded fifty miles in a day. By the time we got to the Sheep Mountains, many of our horses, which hadn't been ridden the entire winter, were still building their stamina. Similarly, our adult riders were still getting into shape. In addition, nearly half our riders were kids, twelve or under. So it was not far-fetched to think an in-shape warrior on an in-shape horse could go a hundred miles a day.

The following day, after checking with a farmer, we found vacant BLM land along White Tail Creek.

That night around the campfire, a few of the riders teased me about not riding horseback with my camera, as I said I would. They took turns telling me I was chicken to try. So the following morning I decided to video while on horseback.

A veteran rider from Standing Rock, Manaja Hill, set me up with his tamest horse. He tied its reins together so they would not drag on the ground and trip the horse. That way I could concentrate on filming with my camera while I rode. He informed me the horse was gentle and would stay within the confines of the herd. All I had to do was stay in the saddle.

Once we got going, I found it unnerving to watch where I was going through a camera viewfinder. But I got my footage, anyway. It impressed everyone that I did it, most of all myself. After I finished, I handed my camera to Floyd so I could finish my leg of the ride unencumbered.

Unknown to me, the riders had been watching me with mischievous eyes. As soon as I was without my camera, they took off galloping. My horse, wanting to stay within the confines of the herd, galloped with them. I was not prepared for this. I grabbed the saddle horn and held on for dear life. We rode about a mile at a full gallop—a mile that seemed would never end. I felt I was about to fall the entire time.

Mercifully, it ended.

My white-knuckle ride amused everybody, but me. The riders retold my adventure several times for the rest of our journey. The retelling always resulted in tons of their laughter. I did not think it was that funny. I did not ride again.

To get away from their ribbing, I drove to Broadus, Montana, to scout for our next campsite. Alone. After stopping at a gas station, I entered the station's convenience store and told the woman behind the counter, Theresa Alderman, I was looking for a campsite for our riders. She referred me to a local named Slug Mills.

I went back to camp, picked up Floyd, and we went to meet Slug.

Slug, wise in the ways of his community, was happy to help and found us a field near Boyes, Montana. However, before we could set up our tents, heavy rains fell. We got muddy and soaked. Slug took pity on us and gave us the use of the shower in his cabin to wash.

Unfortunately, there wasn't enough hot water to last past the first couple of showers. Nobody seemed to care. Just getting clean was enough. He also got friends to donate hay bales to feed our horses and proved himself a tremendous help

As we neared the city of Broadus, we encountered heavy and loud machinery at work on the highway. The riders worried all the noise and activity would spook their horses. When we told the road crew we needed to ride through, they stopped work, turned off their machinery, and escorted our riders through their work area. We expressed our gratitude for their sensitivity and concern for our safety.

Once we entered Broadus, we found a place to camp along the Powder River, courtesy of the Charles Russell family. One of the Russell family members came to visit with her two kids. She said she brought them in hopes our riders would do a Lakota dance for them. The request created an awkward moment. Floyd and Doug looked at each other and wondered how to respond. They didn't want to insult a family member of their host.

Understanding this, I broke the silence and told her, "I can do a pretty mean boogaloo." I wanted to help her understand that not all Natives were powwow dancers, and to assume so was inappropriate. Disappointed, she led her kids out of our encampment. The episode spoke to the disconnect and stereotypes that still exist between the races. Maybe someday people will have more interest in what is in each other's hearts, rather than the color of our skins and the stereotypes that engenders.

The next night we camped at a powwow grounds near the Tongue River, in the Northern Cheyenne Reservation.

During the ride, I had been in contact with Karen. She suggested I contact CNN to get the Crazy Horse family an interview on the Larry King Show to discuss the ride.

"Sorry, I've got no time to do that," I told her.

"Would you have any objections if I tried?"

I said, "Go ahead." I heard nothing more about her Larry King idea for a long time.

She also asked to join our ride. So I picked her up two days later at the Billings Airport. I was genuinely happy to see her. We spent the night camping with the riders.

The next morning, I awoke to a ceremony honoring Fast Horse, the rider who comforted the sick horse left behind at the Besler Ranch. The horse died, but Fast Horse made its last hours as comfortable as he could. The ceremony was being held without my prior knowledge, so I had to rush to get my camera ready.

During the ceremony, the riders presented Fast Horse with an eagle feather. Hill, the same man who loaned me his horse for my never-to-be-forgotten ride, led the ceremony. He tied the feather into Fast Horse's hair while they sang an honoring song. Then the riders took turns shaking Fast Horse's hand. Watching this beautiful ceremony unfold brought a lump to my throat. It was great to see compassion rewarded.

Afterwards, I returned to my car to put away my camera. To my dismay, Karen had rearranged my belongings during my absence, to make everything look tidy. However, I now no longer knew where any of my stuff was. It made me mad, so I opted for a walk to cool off.

During my walk, I noticed there were some tipis added to our encampment. I soon learned that some riders from the Standing Rock Reservation had joined us in the middle of the night. From under the shadows of a cottonwood, a rider named Kermit Miner stood over a barbecue, grilling hot dogs. He called out, "Hey, Bill, would you like to join me for a hot dog?"

I was still angry and in no mood to eat a hot dog, so I told him I wasn't hungry.

"Well then, can I talk to you?" he asked.

"Why?"

"I just want to talk to you," he answered almost as though he was apologizing.

I begrudgingly stopped.

"We're leaving this ride, and the Standing Rock riders that just arrived are coming with us. We don't feel the leadership here is doing this ride in the right way. We'd like you to join us and shoot video of us," he propositioned.

"In the right way? What does that mean?"

"We smelled marijuana coming out of the leader's tent, and we can't have that around the youth," he replied.

I knew Floyd, Don, Carl, and Scott smoked marijuana occasionally, but they had been diligent about keeping it out of sight. Obviously, the smell had given them away. However, I wouldn't jeopardize my chance to learn the genuine story of Crazy Horse because somebody smelled the aroma of a joint. Besides, I had smoked marijuana. In Vietnam it was almost a rite of passage. In addition, I liked Floyd, Doug, Don, Scott, and Carl way better.

"Nah, I'm staying where I'm at," I responded.

His eyes shot daggers. "Okay, but we're the real ride. They ain't doing it right."

I rolled my eyes and walked away. Miner and his group left soon after.

Not everyone from Standing Rock left with Miner. Hill and his sons stayed. They had developed a strong bond with Floyd, Doug, and Don and did not want to break it.

That afternoon our remaining riders rode to one of the Lakota's most sacred sites, Deer Medicine Rock. Here,

Riding to honor their grandfathers
Photo by Mark Frethem

Sitting Bull and Crazy Horse had sundanced. The site rests on the land of Jack Bailey, a rancher.

Bailey's family homesteaded on land that later became the Northern Cheyenne Reservation. When the government created the reservation in 1883, they moved most of the Cheyenne people who had returned from Oklahoma onto it. They moved the homesteaders off. The Bailey family was one of them. They gave the Baileys a new parcel of land to replace the old just on the other side of the new reservation's boundary, which was the same land that held the 1876 Sundance grounds.

We spent two days there. During our stay, the riders brought in chokecherry branches to build a sweat lodge. They purchased a plastic tarp to cover the lodge. Once built, Floyd conducted a sweat lodge ceremony. He said it was the first Lakota sweat on the old Sundance grounds since the days of Crazy Horse and Sitting Bull. I was honored to take part.

The following morning Karen and I visited Deer Medicine Rock. Doug said Deer Medicine Rock is where both the future and past are revealed. A spiritual window into time. It was where the great Lakota spiritual leader, Sitting Bull, had his vision carved into the rock declaring victory for his people at the Battle of the Little Bighorn before the battle happened.

Crazy Horse also carved into rock his vision of how he would die. "Owl Rock," near Deer Medicine Rock, has the shape of an owl. The Clown family knew about the Owl Rock prior to my meeting them. Their grandfathers had described it to them in a ceremony prior to their seeing it. When they made the trip to Jack's place, they immediately recognized Crazy Horse's carving when they first saw it.

The carving shows a Lakota in the upper right-hand corner. To the left of the Lakota is a doctor, who they said was Dr. Valentine McGillycuddy, wearing a stethoscope, who had tried to save Crazy Horse's life. Connecting the Lakota and McGillycudy to a third, larger figure, a row of horse tracks arches upward, meaning Crazy Horse (the larger figure) would arrive in this scenario alive.

The Crazy Horse figure showed two stab wounds, in the liver and kidney area. At the bottom of the carving are more horse tracks, but this time arching to the right as though they were lying down, meaning Crazy Horse would leave dead. They lead to a figure representing a soldier holding a bayonet, standing below the aforementioned Lakota.

It was humbling to see how accurate his vision had been, even down to where he got stabbed. Fifteen months after Crazy Horse carved his vision, a Lakota policeman held him while a sol-

dier stabbed him with a bayonet, twice: once in the kidney area and once in the liver area, after they unsuccessfully attempted to lock him in the jailhouse at Fort Robinson. Dr. McGillicudy's efforts to save him failed.

Once our time at the Bailey Ranch ended, the riders mounted up and resumed their journey

Doug and William in the shadow of the Owl Rock Photo by Mark Frethem

to our last campsite, the Busby powwow grounds on the Northern Cheyenne Reservation. There we feasted with several Cheyenne who also shared their fireworks with us. The following morning we began the last leg of the ride.

The grass had stayed green throughout June, for the first time after a decade of drought, giving the horses fresh grass to eat along the way. The ranchers and others blessed us with their generosity by giving us places to camp, and hay for the horses. Still others helped by donating food and drink.

Floyd, Doug, and Don told me the Creator had led us to the Little Bighorn to form a bridge from the past to the present—from their grandfathers to their children to the yet to be born of their Nation.

As our arrival preceded the memorial dedication by three days, we camped west of Reno-Benteen Hill on the Little Bighorn River. This would also be the starting point of their ride through the battlefield to reach the memorial commemorating their grandfathers. Dawn on June 25th, prior to the park gates opening at 8 a.m., was designated as the starting time.

I wanted to be inside the park before they started this once-in-a-lifetime journey. I thought it would be great to have footage of their faces as they entered the battlefield. But how would I get access inside the park at dawn?

After conferring with the park rangers, they suggested I take a dirt road on private land, just northeast of the battlefield. They said it would allow me access into the battlefield before the gate opened. With the sun still shining, I got into my old Chrysler New Yorker to familiarize myself with the route.

The entrance to the road was right across from where Kermit Miner and the Standing Rock riders had camped after arriving at the battlefield, one day after us. Miner and I had not spoken since I turned down his request to join him. I noticed him watching me open the cattle gate to take the private road into the battlefield. I thought nothing of it. After scouting the road, I decided on the spot—this is where I wanted to enter early the next morning.

Upon my return to camp, I found Carl had his four-wheel ATV delivered to our campsite from the rez. He offered to have one of the younger family members drive me into the park. He said I could sit on the back of his ATV and take video of the riders as they rode through the park to the Indian Memorial. It was a superb idea. I accepted. That night I tossed and turned, too excited to sleep.

We left at 5 a.m. so we would be in the right place at daybreak when the ride started. It was exceptionally cold that morning, and my fingers numbed quickly while riding on the back of the ATV. It was good we had taken the ATV, because Miner had parked two full-sized vehicles in front of the cattle gate sometime the previous night, blocking access to any car wanting to enter the battle-field. To me it was an indication that a Power beyond our own, was taking care of us, just as the riders said. We zipped through the narrow passage between the two vehicles and drove the length of the battlefield to the place I needed to be.

As dawn broke, the skies were overcast.

Once I got my camera in place, I watched the riders send a lone rider across the Little Bighorn River to measure the water's depth. When he made it across without getting soaked, the rest of the riders followed, single file.

As they rode up from the river, I could see the concentration on their faces as they coaxed their horses up the steep hill onto the battlefield. I could hear their horses breathing heavily, and the dense, chilly air made their breath visible.

During their climb, the sun burned through the clouds. Once at the top, the riders rested a moment to absorb its warmth and capture a memory they would cherish their entire lives. Sitting proudly erect, they resumed the ride.

Their grandfathers had held the Americans at bay for nearly seventy years. Their people had beaten Custer's renowned army on the very ground they were crossing.

Historians from other cultures had given all kinds of excuses as to why Custer lost. They said it was because the

Riding up the hill after crossing the Little Bighorn River
Photo by Mark Frethem

soldier's guns didn't work. Or that the soldiers were drunk. They said the soldiers were worn out from no sleep. Excuse after excuse. However, the riders knew the actual truth. The soldiers did not lose the battle. Their grandfathers had won it. To them, it was an honor to honor them. Sitting on the back of the ATV, I could see the unmistakable pride in their faces.

As they approached the memorial they stopped. Some of their relatives walked out to greet them. There were no words. Only feelings of pride and heartfelt jubilance.

When they resumed their ride, several Natives shouted whoops and trills of joy. It sent chills of pride for them down my back. With heads held high, they rode to join Orville Looking Horse, the keeper of the Lakota Nation's sacred calf pipe, for a private ceremony.

My journey across the plains with these riders taught me more about the Lakota and their way of life than any book ever could. It had forced me to stop seeing them through the eyes of a researcher and allowed me to walk a few steps in their shoes. Invaluable.

Riding with pride to the Indian Memorial
Photo by Mark Frethem

Filming Looking Horse's private ceremony was prohibited. So, with nothing further to video, I left for the ranger's office to learn what other events were scheduled.

On the way, I ran into Ernie LaPointe, Sitting Bull's great grandson. He was wearing a ball cap proclaiming himself a Vietnam Veteran. We had met only briefly the night before. Ernie's great grandfather was a great Lakota spiritual leader. He preferred to use the term "great" with grandfather. He did not live on the rez, and it meant less explaining of how he was related to Sitting Bull when talking to his neighbors. So in deference to how he characterized his relationship, I will use the term "great" just as Ernie does. I hoped that at some point I would hear his oral history and maybe deepen my understanding of the Lakota culture. I knew my dad would have wanted me to do that.

Ernie was all smiles. His train of dialog alternated between telling jokes and lambasting the government for sending him to Vietnam. He said he suffered from PTSD.

Then he made an observation, "You must be a Vietnam Veteran."

I had said nothing about having served in Vietnam, so I asked him how he knew.

"Because you have PTSD, too."

I had never considered myself a victim, and I told him I didn't have PTSD.

He persisted.

Finally I asked, "How do you know?"

"I just do," he answered.

Without being able to come up with a specific reason other than his gut feel, I shrugged it off.

I informed him I made documentaries, and if he wanted, I could make one on Sitting Bull based on his family's oral history. He said he would think about it. We exchanged phone numbers. As I turned to go, he reminded me I needed to get my PTSD checked out. I only shook my head in wonder at his persistence.

In the meantime, with Looking Horse's private ceremony over, I wandered over to the Indian Memorial to check it out.

Once inside the memorial, I found a section for each Native Nation that took part in the battle. In the Lakota section, there was a portion honoring Sitting Bull and a portion honoring Crazy Horse.

The Crazy Horse section included the lines written by Floyd for the park service on behalf of his family. It was humbling and beautiful to see his words come to life on the wall. It read: "Tashunke Witko, Minikouju Lakota,

"In memoriam to members of the Lakota band of the great Sioux Nation. The Cut Head, Two Kettle, Blackfeet, Minikouju, Hunkpapa, No Bow, Flathead. Also the Nakota, Dakota bands of the Great Sioux Nation, Cheyenne Nation, and Arapaho Nation who fought here on the battlefield against the United States 7th Army. The battle was fought because the United States wanted the Black Hills and its natural resources. The United States declared war, stipulating violations by the Great Sioux Nation regarding articles of law of the United States.

"Our grandfather, Tashunke Witko, fought in this battle to preserve a way of life, Nature's Law for the Lakota Oyate. Nature's Law applies to all mankind, no matter what race. The Nations present had their own culture, language, and traditions that guide their everyday life.

Our grandfathers protected our sacred pipe because it was given to us by the Creator, God, believing that all mankind was given the power of truth, justice, and wisdom. All warriors at the battle that were killed believed in this way of living life. Our grandfathers say that the Cheyenne, Arapaho came because they had family ties with the Lakota Nation.

"Our grandfather, Tashunke Witko, was a man that prayed with the sacred pipe, played with the children and listened to the elders. He saw that all living things were higher than him because he knew that mankind had the power of choice to do right or wrong, good or bad. So we must pray for the truth and honesty to help mankind. Our grandfathers told us that all mankind were created equal and they represent the earth man with no skin color. So mankind must get together to right the wrongs done in our lifetime. We the family of Tashunke Witko have the highest honor for all that were involved in the battle and their descendants in order to heal our Grandmother the Earth we unify through peace.

"Pilamaye le Un Nib'ki,

"Thank you we live,

"Tashunke Witko Tiwahe, Minikouju Lakota."

A few years later, the park service changed his words on the mural in collaboration with a tribal official without Floyd's or the Crazy Horse family's permission. It no longer says that the United States declared war on the Lakota. Upon realizing the change, Floyd commented, "They sugarcoated it." Yet they still attributed the altered quote to his family. It is a prime example of how history changes to suit the dominant culture.

Floyd Clown speaks at the Little Bighorn Battlefield
(left to right): Donlan Many Bad Horses, Park Superintendent
Darrell J. Cook, Floyd, and Kitty Deernose
Photo by Mark Frethem

That afternoon, several speakers praised the Indian Memorial dedication. Ernie was one of them. He spoke on behalf of the Sitting Bull family.

Don Red Thunder spoke on behalf of the Crazy Horse family. He ended his talk by saying the Crazy Horse family had many members and was still alive and well. He emphasized that Crazy Horse was from the Minikouju band. Then he and other family members and friends sang the Tashunke Witko Song (Crazy Horse Song).

As night fell, we retired to our tents. I knew deep down inside this was a day that would live in my heart forever.

The following morning, I took Karen to the airport and saw her off. Then I packed up with the rest of the riders to go back to the rez. On the way, we stopped at Crazy Horse Mountain to help Ruth, sculptor Korcak Ziolkowski's surviving widow, celebrate her seventy-seventh birthday. All the ambitions that Floyd, Doug, and Don had dreamed in early spring were now a reality. Our riders and the Crazy Horse family gave Ruth a star quilt blanket for her birthday gift. Their gift still adorns the Visitor's Center wall at the Crazy Horse Mountain complex, as of this writing.

They also told Ruth how their family was involved with her husband from the beginning. The way they agreed to the carving was only if the US government was never to be a part of it. They allowed Ziolkowski to use two of Iron Cedar's sons, Joseph and James Clown, and a photo of Moses Clown as models for the carving's face. Ruth told the family she had never asked, nor did Korcak ever say, how he had come up with the face. She thanked the family for the fresh information.

After the birthday celebration, I happened to see Doug and Don's mom, Beverly Clown. She had come to attend the birthday celebration with the riders. She smiled a smile of acceptance at me. I smiled back. It was further proof in my mind that I was gaining the family's trust to be able to tell their story.

Following our day at Crazy Horse Mountain, we went home. Once back at Floyd's, we partook in a sweat. After the sweat, they gave me the special privilege of smoking and praying with Crazy Horse's sacred pipe.

The pipe has a long stem that stretched from my shoulder to my fingertips. I could not touch it except with my lips to smoke it. Floyd held the pipe as each participant took a few puffs.

It was an honor that stays with me to this very day.

The family vowed to continue the ride for the next three years, to total four trips. Four is a sacred number in the Lakota culture.

When the time came for me to leave, I didn't want to go. But I had to get back. I was running out of funds.

As I began my drive home, my cell phone rang.

Chapter Nine

Homeless

ERNIE CALLED TO SAY he received a letter from Bill Billeck, Program Director at the Smithsonian Repatriation office in Washington, DC. They said they had a lock
of Sitting Bull's hair and his leggins in their possession.
Ernie told me he was shocked.

Billeck informed him that under a law called the
Native American Graves Protection and Repatriation Act,
any institution receiving
federal money had to
return all Native Amer-
ican remains and pat-
rimonial objects to the
closest living relative. In
his capacity at the Smithsonian, it was Billeck's
job to return Sitting Bull's
lock of hair, considered a
body part, and leggins,

Ernie and Bill

taken without permission from his corpse, back to Sitting Bull's closest relatives.

Ernie and his sisters knew themselves to be the closest living relatives, and entered a claim. Eventually, Ernie and Billeck arranged to meet at Ernie's house in Lead, South Dakota, on July 22, 2003. They would discuss Ernie's evidence validating his family's status.

Ernie didn't trust the government. Since the Smithsonian is government funded, he asked if I would document the meeting on video so he would have something to fall back on, in case Billeck tried to trick him. He also requested I ask Floyd, Doug, and Don to attend as witnesses on his behalf.

The meeting would take place around Ernie's dining room table. Ernie's wife, Sonja, his sister Ethel Little Spotted Horse Bates, and her husband, Scott, were also to be in attendance, along with a few additional friends and family. I agreed to go. Floyd, Doug, and Don also honored his request to be there.

Once I arrived, Ernie pulled me aside to warn me about his sister Ethel. "Our Aunt Sarah, who raised Ethel, never learned anything about Sitting Bull. She used to sneak away to spend time with boys whenever she and my mom, Angeline, were offered the opportunity to listen to a telling of Sitting Bull's stories by Standing Holy. Standing Holy was their mother and Sitting Bull's daughter. So Ethel hasn't heard any family stories and knows very little. I think you should keep your camera pointed at me and Billeck."

Billeck arrived dressed for business. He had the demeanor of an attorney. After introductions, he explained that when they murdered Sitting Bull, the Army

Bill Billeck

surgeon and undertaker at Fort Yates, Dr. Horace Deeble, had stolen a braid of Sitting Bull's hair (his scalp lock) as a souvenir. He also took Sitting Bull's leggins. Six years after stealing them, he loaned them to the Smithsonian Museum so they could be displayed for the world to see. The museum never heard from him again. Rather than display the scalp lock, the Smithsonian placed it into a file folder and forgot about it. Now, over a century later while rummaging through old files, the museum had re-discovered it.

They searched for Sitting Bull's closest living relatives so they could return the items and stay in compliance with the Native American Graves Protection and Repatriation Act. They sent inquiry letters to the reservations as part of the search. They consulted tribal elders. They searched archives. As a result, two claims were submitted.

Ernie and his sisters submitted one claim. The other was from Don Tenoso, a descendant of Sitting Bull's nephew, One Bull. Tenoso claimed Sitting Bull adopted One Bull in a Lakota Hunka (making a relative) Ceremony as his son—thus, putting him on equal footing with Ernie and his sisters.

Upon hearing this, Ernie expressed incredulity, "Tenoso's dead wrong!"

Ernie then laid out his own proof of how he and his sister's lineage connected directly to Sitting Bull. Billeck studied it and said it impressed him. However, he refused to declare Ernie and his sisters as the closest relatives. He said he still had to investigate Tenoso's claim.

Ernie shot Billeck a look of disbelief and told Billeck in no uncertain terms that Sitting Bull would never have made One Bull his son in a Hunka Ceremony. The Hunka Ceremony is for making someone a relative, not a specific kind of relative. Thus, if One Bull was already a blood relation, it was nonsense for the ceremony to be held at all.

Billeck repeated he still had to check out Tenoso's claim and then asked Ernie how he felt about sharing the lock and leggins with Tenoso.

Ernie responded emphatically that he would never share them with Tenoso. He claimed One Bull helped set the wheels in motion to murder his great grandfather, and as a descendant of One Bull, Tenoso had blood on his hands. And the only way to wash the blood off his hands was to agree to a Wiping of the Tears Ceremony. (I understood this as a ceremony of apology to Ernie and his sisters by the relatives of One Bull for their family member taking part in the killing of their great grandfather).

Billeck then sighed and informed Ernie he would take his argument into consideration, excused himself, and left.

We sat in silence for a moment. Ernie was angry. He asked anybody and everybody in the room, "Why did he even come if he wasn't going to award me and my sisters our great grandfather's hair and leggings?"

We greeted his question with silence. We didn't know.

I suggested to Ernie I keep the videotapes of our meeting in case he needed to use them later. He nodded. However, with no promises made, we both knew they most likely would have no value.

Before leaving, I reintroduced my proposal of collaborating on a documentary about his great grandfather. Since the Crazy Horse brothers had not committed to doing one on Crazy Horse yet, I hoped Ernie would do one on Sitting Bull. He demurred. He was in no mood to consider it. So I left.

Once home, I was ready to edit the Little Bighorn ride documentary. Because the riders had done their journey with so much faith and passion, I proposed calling it "Journey of the Heart." Floyd, Doug, and Don agreed.

Upon reviewing my footage, I found the sound was of poor quality, and I approached an audio friend in Portland, Mark Frethem, who had worked with me on my ill-fated musical feature film. I asked if he would help make the audio presentable. He accepted, and he became a co-producer on it. We agreed to share any proceeds we got with the Great Sioux Nation Victory Ride over the upcoming three years.

While editing, I took breaks to refresh my brain. The breaks gave me time to join an internet chat room frequented by several Battle of the Little Bighorn historians.

When I introduced the fact Floyd, Doug, and Don represented the family of the only living relatives to Crazy Horse, and Ernie and his sisters were the closest living relatives to Sitting Bull, most in the chat room did not take me seriously. They were unwilling to deviate from what they had found from their own research and readings.

I got the impression many of them felt I lacked the pedigree to contradict their findings, which were mostly regurgitations of what had already been written. Some insinuated most claims made by Natives were unreliable. Some even referred to Native oral history as "oral tradition," as though the Native tellings lacked the credibility to earn the label of "history."

They regarded government documents like the *Crazy Horse Surrender Ledger* (a ledger book of names recorded by government employees of those who surrender) as gospels of truth. But Floyd, Doug, and Don, among other Lakota, knew differently. Only 300 of the approximately 900 names who were recorded in the ledger were warriors that rode with Crazy Horse. The rest greeted Crazy Horse prior to entering the Red Cloud Agency and rode into the agency with him. Since they were with him when he arrived, the government employees assumed they were Crazy Horse's people and recorded them into the ledger. Those recorded received an extra serving of rations and blankets—an incentive not lost on those who greeted other surrendering groups that followed.

In Ernie's case, Sitting Bull's daughter knew her father as only a daughter could, so when she passed information to her daughter Angeline, it came from listening to her father's first-hand accounts. She had the knowledge to explain anything about him Angeline didn't understand. Angeline also heard it without the additional baggage of a translator, who most likely would be a stranger to Sitting

Bull and his family. A translator who could translate words but not the proper context.

The same was true with the Clown family. Crazy Horse's youngest sister, Iron Cedar, told their family's oral history to her son Edward, who told it to his youngest son, Floyd, and grandsons, Doug and Don. There was no need to hear it through a third party.

Ernie and the Clown family knew their family's stories in English and Lakota. They could verify whether a retelling of these stories was accurate in either language. Something Black Elk, in the book "Black Elk Speaks" by John Neihardt, could not do because Black Elk didn't know English. He could not proofread the book to ensure accuracy, even though it had his name on it. The same could be said about other influential translations, like those of the Cheyenne warrior Woodenleg's stories by an American, Thomas Marquis. They weren't proofread because they were in English and not their Native tongues. Yet many historians viewed them as more accurate than what each of these two families knew about their own family's journey.

Some historians even discounted these stories because they felt they should have been told sooner, as though the earlier known stories somehow had more validity. Anyone who understands the Lakota knows nature and spirituality is what drives their culture. Not a calendar. The calendar and the keeping of time was an obsession brought to North America by European immigrants. In the Lakota culture, it is up to the person or family to pick the time when they want to tell their story—not society.

During one heated chat room discussion, I asked a historian named Ephraim Dickson, who was planning a trip to the Cheyenne River Reservation to meet a friend, if he would meet with a Clown family member to verify the information I was posting and then report back to the chat room. I wanted them to know what I was telling them was real. He said he would. Doug was the family member I arranged for him to meet. Doug would present his paperwork and family death certificates proving his family's claim.

The historian drove to the Cheyenne River Reservation from Utah. However, upon completing his visit with his friend, he posted that the Clown family was not related to Crazy Horse.

When I questioned Doug about what had happened at their meeting, he told me the historian never even met with him.

The historian had broken a promise. Not only had he not met with Doug, but he had not seen the family's paperwork or death certificates. Yet he was reporting the Clowns were unrelated *as though* he had seen Doug's paperwork. The fact they didn't meet was absent from his post.

According to Doug, this historian's friend even said he had pointed Doug out to him. The historian declined to even say hello. Instead, Doug said the historian got into his jeep and drove home.

After that episode, my respect for historians diminished. Not all historians want to find truth. The only thing many of them seek is evidence collaborating their own established viewpoint. Then they feed their families by getting people to believe their viewpoint and regard them as "experts." And as I had learned from my Vietnam days, there is no such thing as an "expert."

So I doubled down. I would not let these valuable family stories be discredited by people with agendas. I stayed up entire nights refuting chat room arguments made against the family's stories. One positive that came from this was it helped me refine my ability to communicate the family's information in a better way.

For instance, Ernie said his family moved from the Standing Rock Reservation to the Pine Ridge Reservation not long after Sitting Bull's murder. The so-called experts were adamant that the closest Sitting Bull family members had not moved to Pine Ridge but still lived in Standing Rock. They also argued the closest Crazy Horse descendants were still on Pine Ridge. I pointed out the whole scenario made little sense. The Standing Rock Indian police had murdered Sitting Bull, while tribal members from the Red Cloud Agency (now Pine Ridge Reservation), had helped murder Crazy Horse. If only they could imagine themselves in a family member's shoes. After all, if the head of your family is murdered by your neighbors, do you stay in the same neighborhood? I have asked that question over one hundred times of various people from many backgrounds, and the answer has always been no. The only exception was when one individual I asked said they would only stay if they aligned themselves with the murderers. I often wondered why these historians had not incorporated that simple logic into their thinking.

During this time, I kept in contact with Ernie. I continued to pester him about doing a documentary on his great grandfather. But he still hesitated.

Finally, one day he asked, "How would you go about making this documentary?"

"You tell your oral history and I'll capture it on video. Then I'll shoot some footage to help support your oral history."

"How do I know it will come out the way I told it?" Ernie persisted.

"You can watch the finished movie before it's released, and if you see something that needs to be changed, I'll change it."

Ernie praying at Bear Butte

I wanted this to be Ernie's oral history. I wanted to leave as light a footprint as possible. Leaving a bigger footprint would be a disservice to not only Ernie but to present and future generations who wanted to know his family's story.

Ernie thought it over, and after a few days he agreed and invited me to stay at his and Sonja's residence in the spring of 2004 while we filmed our documentary.

I was elated.

During the winter months prior to going to live at Ernie's place, I sold trucks and SUVs. Or at least tried. I had taken a job as a salesman at Northside Ford Trucks in Portland. The sales manager there felt that everybody who visited our car lot should buy a vehicle before they left, no matter what.

I didn't mind selling cars. I just had a hard time with the "no matter what" part. I am not a good pressure salesman. In fact, I turned out to be an utter failure at it. But one excellent thing came out of it. I bought a used, four-wheel-drive Ford Explorer—sales commission free. I could now go places I could not before.

When spring arrived, I quit my job and drove to Ernie's place. I had little money, but I figured I could pay my way by working in neighboring Deadwood. It was a summer tourist town, and only ten minutes from Ernie's.

Unfortunately, once I moved there, I discovered Deadwood paid starvation wages.

In early May I got my first job offer in Deadwood. It paid $6.50 per hour. I considered it an insult and declined, though I kept applying at other places. Another two weeks went by. No better offers. Close to broke, I swallowed my pride and took a job at a casino named Goldberg's making hamburgers and scooping ice cream for $6.50 per hour.

Ernie was a passionate person, with a touch of an entertainer in him. We engaged in several stimulating conversations. He would alternate between trashing the government and telling delightfully funny and insightful stories.

In one conversation, Ernie told me there were no Hunkpapas any more. The Hunkpapa was the band of the Lakota that Sitting Bull had belonged to. He told me a spirit had told him this during a ceremony, that's how he knew it to be true.

His assertion sounded similar to what Floyd had said about the Oglala and Sicangu bands. That they, just as Ernie stated about the Hunkpapas, were illegitimate. It gave me a fresh perspective on why they disagreed with the generally accepted, present-day list of Lakota bands.

Floyd's and Ernie's truths were passed down orally, before their birth. The fact that the Oglala and Sicangu had acted on the government's behalf in eliminating Crazy Horse—and the Hunkpapa had done the same with Sitting Bull—all most likely played a role in their perspectives. Why wouldn't their earlier descendants be bitter over what had happened and banished those bands from the Lakota Nation in their stories? Yet my heart told me to stand tough before I accepted this premise as fact. Maybe these facts were totally unrelated. There could be things to come I didn't know about. So, I kept my mind open and ready to receive new facts—not rush to judgment.

I also learned that Ernie had been warned by his mom not to tell others he was related to Sitting Bull. She said it would change his life, and maybe not for the better. It was similar to what the Clowns told me about their being warned not reveal their lineage.

My conversations with Ernie became less frequent once he found out where I worked and what I was doing. I think it affected his confidence in my abilities. I would have felt the same way if I had been in his shoes. A hamburger flipper making a polished documentary on his great grandfather? It sounds absurd, even as I write it now. He had no time for any interviews before the camera. He always had a reason he couldn't make himself available. No matter when or how I asked.

During that time, I had the wonderful fortune to reconnect with one of my Bravo platoon buddies from Vietnam, Guy Dull Knife Jr., whom I had known only as "Chief" in Vietnam. Reading a book called, *The Dull Knives of Pine Ridge*, by Joe Starita, had helped me make the connection that Chief, who I served with, was Guy Dull Knife Jr.

When I first joined Bravo, another Lakota named Francis Whitebird helped me fill my medic bag because he said he wanted me to pay special attention to Chief. Whitebird, who had been the head medic for Bravo prior to my arrival as a substitute for Doc Elliott.

Dull Knife lived in Wambli, South Dakota. Floyd accompanied me when I met him. After our joyful reunion, he honored me with an eagle feather in recognition of my service in Vietnam. He also showed me some of his artwork along with a beautifully carved pipe he had made. The pipe had an intricately carved buffalo near the pipe's bowl. I have never seen a better carved pipe, and I have seen many.

Guy told me he had married a member of the Chipps family. He claimed he was not very popular with his in-laws because he had divorced one of their daughters to marry another daughter from the same family. The family had four daughters in all. He said every time he saw one of the two remaining daughters, he told them he would marry them next. The Chipps family did not think it as funny as he did. Unfortunately, Guy passed away on October 31, 2019.

In early June, I got a call from Don asking if I would video the Great Sioux Nation Victory Ride's second year. The value of remaking a documentary I had already finished was questionable. But I agreed to their request in case I changed my mind.

When I arrived at the Clown cemetery for their second ride, I found the planned start to be more elaborate than the previous year's ride. They brought in an entire drum group to sing. The riders lined up, side by side. Upon a pre-arranged signal, they rode in one long, parallel line. It was well choreographed and striking... but then the worst thing that could happen happened... my camera jammed.

This had never happened before. At least not with my JVC camcorder. The scenes they had so painstakingly set up for me to shoot, I could not record.

I apologized and left feeling devastated. I tried fixing the camera at Ernie's place and found I could not. So I sent it to a repair shop in California. Sonja, out of the goodness of her heart, agreed to put the repairs on her credit card as long as I paid her back.

I now had no camera to shoot Ernie's documentary. I realized that working at Goldberg's wouldn't pay enough to support my needs and also pay Sonja back. It didn't pay enough to keep my documentary ambitions alive or my ability to pay Karen's credit card payments on the camera. So I took a second job as a cashier at a casino named B.B. Cody's at the slightly better pay of $7.00 per hour. By this time, I had learned it was common for people working in Deadwood to have two jobs to make ends meet.

Recognizing my financial plight, Ernie again suggested I get checked out for PTSD at the Veteran's Administration. He said he was sure I had it. He added once their psychiatrists diagnosed me with it, I could get monthly disability payments like he got. Disability payments that allowed him to own his own home and eat well.

I wasn't sold. I did not believe I was suffering from post-war trauma. I considered myself to be normal. Besides, I did not trust psychiatrists.

One day he asked if I would come with him to the Veteran's Administration to have my old war wounds checked out. He convinced me to see if I was still eligible for any compensation. To relieve some tension that had been building between us because of my stubbornness in not wanting to see any shrinks, I relented. I still felt occasional sharp pains in my upper left thigh where two pieces of shrapnel had lodged against my thigh bone. And if the government was willing to pay bonuses for getting shot, that was something I could accept.

During our visit to the VA, the official we met said he would check and see if the case for my war wounds was still open. If it was and I had discomfort, the doctors might award me compensation. He said he would get back to me. At that point I figured the meeting was over, so I rose and extended my hand for a parting handshake when Ernie spoke.

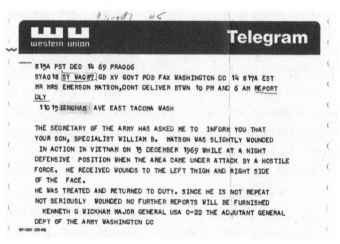

Army telegram hand delivered to William's family after being wounded in Vietnam. The telegram says "slightly," but the wound was a piece of mortar shrapnel in his temple and two large pieces of shrapnel resting against his thigh bone. It infected, and he stayed in the hospital for two months.

"I think they should check him for PTSD, too. I know he has it."

My heart sank.

I didn't want to object and put Ernie and myself at odds in front of a stranger. So I said nothing.

The next thing I knew, I had an appointment to see a VA shrink—actually two VA shrinks. They scheduled regular weekly appointments with me for the next two months. I was to see each shrink separately.

After attending those sessions, the first shrink suggested that I was bi-polar and he could cure me by prescribing a medicine that would even out my highs and lows. I declined his medication and told him life is full of highs and lows, and I wanted my mind to be awake even during my emotional swings. I wanted to live my life fully. My reaction miffed him. He never treated me with the same respect again.

The other shrink was less forthcoming with his thoughts and harder to read.

I had gone to see them while working eighty hours a week. Unfortunately, working that many hours and spending time with the shrinks left me no time to concentrate on the documentary.

In late June, I received an email from Karen asking where I was living. I found it to be a strange question because I had already told her I was staying at Ernie and Sonja's place. I wondered why she would think I would move and not tell her.

I found out the next day.

Sonja requested we talk. During that talk, she asked me to leave their house. She told me to return to Tacoma and stay with my mom, because she and Ernie saw no future in working with me.

It hurt, but I understood her point.

They had cared for me. Cooked my meals. Tolerated my habits. In return, I was to deliver a documentary. I had made no progress other than a few wildlife shots. With no progress on our documentary, I had become a burden. It broke my heart, and I moved out with tears of failure streaming down my cheeks.

However, their belief that I needed to run home to Mom was disturbing. The more I thought about it, the more my resolve stiffened. I had never considered myself a quitter, and I would not start now because Sonja had suggested it. I still had the ability to do a documentary. Maybe I needed to re-approach Floyd, Doug, and Don instead. It would be harder because of the five-hour, roundtrip drive to the rez and my schedule being so packed. But it was worth a try.

So I stayed in the Black Hills and lived out of my car. I continued to work in Deadwood. I told Sonja and Ernie of my decision, and they seemed surprised. During subsequent conversations, Ernie told me Karen had proposed getting them on the Larry King Show and helping them with the Sitting Bull documentary since I was so busy working.

For whatever reason, she had never told me of these conversations and now it seemed she had become a competitor.

When I confronted Karen about it, she denied it. However, after living with Ernie and Sonja, I knew their television habits did not include the Larry King Show. I had never heard them even talk about it. It had been Karen who had talked about it. She had wanted Floyd, Doug, and Don to go on his show the previous spring. It was obvious she had presented Ernie with the same proposition.

I still owed her for the camera, so I kept my thoughts to myself—at least until I paid her off.

Chapter Ten

The Grandfathers

A FORESTED HILL OVERLOOKING Deadwood was my new home. I parked my car there at night to sleep. I inflated my air mattress and unrolled my sleeping bag in the back of my SUV. My bedding competed with my belongings. It was crowded.

Each morning I showered for a dollar at the Deadwood Recreation Center so I would look and smell presentable. I remained numb over my eviction. Ernie and Sonja had accepted me as their guest while completing our documentary. However, our common goal didn't happen quickly enough, and I was naïve to think there would be no consequences.

Thankfully, I had my camera back from the repair shop, so I still had the possibility of doing *something*. I just had to figure out what that something was.

My job as casino cashier at B. B. Cody's required me to make complimentary popcorn and serve free soft drinks to those who gambled, make change, and pay off winners.

My meals were comprised of the free soft drinks I served and the complimentary popcorn I popped. Not particularly a healthy diet, but it kept me alive.

Ernie stopped by the casino occasionally to see how I was doing. To me, it was a sign there was still hope for us to finish what we started.

Prior to staying with Ernie, I had ordered one thousand DVDs of *Journey of the Heart*. Although the Cheyenne River Sioux Tribe financed the second year of the family's ride to the battlefield, there was no guarantee the riders would get their next two years financed to fulfill their four-year commitment. The tribe was often broke. This motivated Floyd, Doug, Don, and myself to sell the videos so we could make enough money to ensure the ride would continue all four years. Our first DVD signing was in Deadwood's Adams Museum, around mid-July.

When we met after not having seen each other for months, it was a joyous occasion. However, when I told them my new living arrangements, they responded with some harsh words about Ernie. I told them I was to blame for not producing a video in a timely fashion, but they would have none of that. Unfortunately, this became a prelude to a rivalry between them and Ernie that would have to be tolerated for a long time.

Our event went well. Ernie came by to show his support. I appreciated his presence.

After the signing, I had to go back to work at Goldberg's. Floyd, Doug, and Don accompanied me there and ate where I worked. After their supper, I took a break and approached them about doing a documentary on their oral history. We had discussed it before, but the result was

William working at Goldberg's

filming the ride instead. This time they were open to it, and that's all I needed to hear.

I came up with several ideas, however they supported a single idea—a documentary on their family tree. It didn't sound nearly as exciting as a battle or another major event in Crazy Horse's life, but I agreed and shifted my thinking.

I decided to video some sites where their ancestors had lived. I wanted to make their family history as complete as possible. One of their ancestors' sites was along the Owl River. On a map, it is the Moreau River. I went there to capture some video. When I arrived, the grass and reeds bordering the little river were knee-high and blocked my view of the water. I maneuvered myself to the river bank so I could get the best shot possible. Suddenly, two huge owls flew out of the reeds from about six feet in front of me. It startled me so much that the hair on the back of my neck stood up. One flew to the opposite bank and perched on a rock. He watched me while the other one disappeared. This experience made me realize why the Lakota called this the Owl River. Their names told what was there. The Americans had changed the name to honor a French trader, but the trader's name said nothing about what was there.

That's when I understood that the renaming of rivers and other landmarks has led to a subtle disconnect from the land, without people realizing it. Naming of our rivers and land formations holds great importance for the Natives, but the US government, in their rush to re-name them, were blind to how they were erasing a long-term history and knowledge of the land.

Suddenly I felt a deep desire to learn all the original Lakota names for the waterways and landmarks. I wanted to reconnect to the land as much as possible and help others do the same. Floyd, Doug, and Don were my resources. The Yellowstone River was originally the Elk River, because it was a popular watering hole for the elk. The Cheyenne River was the Good River, because the water was clear and tasted good (today it is not so clear). The Grand River was the River That Was Bigger Than Its Banks, because it often flooded—to name a few. A more complete list can now be found in the pages of *Crazy Horse: The Lakota Warrior's Life and Legacy*.

Later that summer, I took a job at the Franklin Hotel as a slot technician. Today, this work has mostly been replaced by technological advances. Then, it paid eight dollars an hour, a fortune compared to Goldberg's. I quit Goldberg's but kept my job at B. B. Cody's, until my paycheck bounced. Angry, I felt I had no choice but to quit and concentrate on working at the Franklin. By cutting down on my work hours, I had more time to video, though less for gas money.

It cost a full tank of gas to go to the Cheyenne River Rez. So, to save money, I stayed closer to home and concentrated on filming wildlife at Custer State Park in Custer, South Dakota. I planned on using the shots to juxtapose against the family's oral history. Because their way of life was being one with nature, this was an obvious choice.

One sunny day in late July, I went to Custer Park to shoot. I had already captured deer, buffalo, prairie dogs, pronghorn, and elk, but had yet to capture video of male bighorn sheep with their distinctive curled horns.

I asked a park ranger where I might find bighorn rams. He told me they last saw some along a road known as the Needles Highway. I hopped in my car and drove that route. After a few miles, I stumbled upon six bighorn rams peacefully munching grass. I got out of my car and ended up sitting among them. To my surprise, they accepted me as though I was one of them. Some even laid down less than a yard from me. As a result, I got some terrific shots and felt a deep fellowship with them. I used these shots in my documentaries.

My life began to stabilize. I had paid enough of what I owed Sonja and Karen that I could see a light at the end of tunnel. I had also finished all my sessions with the two shrinks at the VA. Now they were asking me to see their head shrink. I did not feel optimistic anything would come of it. Besides, they were robbing me of time I could spend videoing wildlife. But I went.

On my first visit to the head psychiatrist, he was late. When he finally showed up, it became an abbreviated get-to-know-you session. On my second appointment, the receptionist told me they had called him away on an emergency, and he would see me as soon as he could. A pattern seemed to be emerging. I waited. When he didn't show after about fifteen minutes, I had had enough. I walked out of the reception area and headed to my car. I was about to open my car door when the head psychiatrist and the receptionist yelled at me to stop from the door of the building.

I paused.

When they finally reached me, the head psychiatrist couldn't help but see my sleeping bag and air mattress in the back.

"Where are you going? You have an appointment," the receptionist stated.

"He was taking too long," I replied.

"I apologize, but please come back in. I can help you," the head shrink pleaded.

"I don't really need your help," I countered. I really didn't think he could help.

Then he focused on my bedding, "Where are you living?"

Knowing he had seen my sleeping bag and air mattress, my stoic and angry exterior broke, and I admitted I was living out of my car.

"Come inside, we need to talk about this. Maybe I can make things better," he said gently.

As I walked back to the building, tears rolled down my cheeks. I found pride a hard thing to swallow.

Once in his office, he asked, "Why didn't you tell anyone you were living out of your car?"

My answer was simple. Nobody had asked. He then apologized on behalf of his department and told me he would help me get a roof over my head ASAP.

I initially found his statement suspect, but I must admit, he kept his word.

Within a few weeks, they had diagnosed me with PTSD. Since my PTSD was not considered to be a danger to myself or anyone else, any therapy I was to receive would be strictly voluntary. I never volunteered for any.

Ernie had been right. I would now receive enough compensation for me to move into a motel at a weekly rate until I found an apartment.

In late August, the VA assigned me to have my war wounds examined at the Hot Springs VA Medical Center. I spent the night there. The medical staff had me perform several exercises to see what kind of mobility I had in the leg that took the mortar shrapnel. When the examination was done, they awarded me additional disability—all the way back to 1970, the day I left the service. It wasn't a huge check, but more than I'd seen in a long time.

With that, I felt whole. I called Doug and arranged for him and his brothers to come to Portland so we could record their oral history in a studio where the sound would be pristine.

However, before they left to visit me, I went to see them. Floyd invited me to sweat.

The night was clear and cool. The Milky Way was bright and vivid. The air was fresh and clean. Just as in previous sweats, we undressed, stood out of respect for the filling of the pipe and the song that accompanied it. We said "Mitakuye Oyasin" and entered Floyd's new Bear Lodge. They brought in the red-hot rocks. The sweat lodge door was closed.

The rocks seemed brighter that night. As Floyd poured water over them, images emerged and rose to shoulder level. As they came into focus, I beheld a semi-circle of elder male Natives sitting and staring into the rocks. Blankets covered their naked shoulders. There were five of them. I saw them in detail. The one on the far left was facing in a way that I could see the profile of his face. They did not speak or acknowledge my presence.

I wanted to tell someone, but I did not want to interrupt the ceremony, so I kept my excitement inside of me.

Once the first round was over, and the door opened, the elder Natives disappeared. At this point I wondered if I had seen what I thought I had seen. Maybe it was just my angle that made me think I saw them. I adjusted the angle I was sitting and shut my eyes tight to erase what I might have seen. Upon closing the door once again and re-opening my eyes for the second round, they reappeared.

Now I was convinced.

Their presence continued through all four rounds. Once we finished the sweat, I could hardly contain myself, and after I emerged from the sweat lodge, I told everybody what I had seen. I expected them to be as surprised as I was.

They weren't.

"We already know what you saw," stated Floyd. "You doubted us, so the grandfathers showed themselves to you."

They were right. I had questioned the fact that the entire Lakota Nation would sweat with their family, among other things. Now they showed me a part of their world I could no longer deny.

Two years later I saw the same Native that sat on the far left in a drawing from an out-of-print book (at the time) from the 1930s, *Custer's Conqueror* by William Bordeaux. He had labeled his drawing as Crazy Horse, but

Floyd, Doug, and Don knew the drawing was actually Old Man Crazy Horse, or Waglula. I felt honored, finding out he was in the sweat with me.

During the entire time I knew them, Floyd, Doug, and Don said they talked to their grandfathers on the other side. After learning their grandfathers were deceased, I didn't put a lot of stock into what they said the grandfathers were telling them. However, after seeing the elders appear from the rocks, plus remembering I heard my dad speaking to me earlier on Bear Butte, I became a believer. I no longer doubted they communicate with their deceased ancestors.

I had seen them with my own eyes.

I kept quiet about this experience for some time. Later, I finally opened up to a neighbor, who was a Christian minister. When I told him about my sweat lodge experience with Old Man Crazy Horse, he dismissed it by saying, "Sometimes Native Americans use drugs in their ceremonies."

Having known what I had seen and knowing I had taken no drugs prior to the sweat, I felt insulted. But in retrospect, I believe he was saying it more for his own benefit than mine. Once back to Portland, I contacted Mark to get a block of time in his recording studio, so we could record more family interviews and Lakota songs for our documentaries.

When my guests arrived, I was eager to show them an excellent time. We drove all over the Northwest and as far south as the Bay Area. We visited Seattle, my mom and brother's family in Tacoma, my sister's family in Washougal, Washington, the Sea Lion Caves on the Oregon Coast, and Diana and Phil Harvey, relatives of Floyd, Doug, and

Don, living in Vallejo, California. They took us to Alcatraz in San Francisco. Doug got to see the ocean for the first time in his life.

During our time at Mark's studio, they impressed me by how well they knew their family tree. It made me think about my own family tree. Prior to conducting the interviews, I thought I knew my family tree extremely well, but after listening to them—I knew I was fooling myself.

I came away from their visit feeling we had taken a giant step forward in gaining an even bigger piece of each other's trust.

Once they went back to the rez, I researched my own tree. I read up on Ralph Waldo Emerson, the famous writer I had been told was my relative. Late in his life,

Don, Doug, William, and Floyd in San Francisco
Photo by Diana Harvey

*William, Floyd, and Mark Frethem relax near
Deer Medicine Rock, 2005*

my dad told me they had named me after Ralph Waldo's brother, William. But I never totally bought into that because I still remembered a trip I took as a youngster to Bill Lohr's Sporting Goods Store, on Aurora Avenue in Seattle. Dad introduced me to the owner, Bill Lohr, and said at the time I was named after Lohr. I think Lohr was giving him a discount on fishing and hunting equipment, and my being named after him was Dad's way of saying thank you. Once we moved to Tacoma, he lost contact with Lohr. He probably figured it was safe to give me a more sophisticated reason for being named William.

My dad inherited an old book from his grandparents called *The History of Fulton County, Illinois*, published in the late 1800s. Its size made Webster's Dictionary look like a pamphlet. My Dad showed me a picture of William Emerson from this book and said it was Ralph Waldo's brother. However, when I researched Ralph Waldo's tree from numerous public records, I found the birth and death dates of his brother did not match with those from Dad's book. I also found Ralph Waldo's brother William had lived most of his life in New York and not Fulton County, Illinois. It was questionable whether Ralph Waldo's brother had even set foot in Illinois.

Had Dad invented a relationship to Ralph Waldo Emerson, hoping to give us a more positive image of ourselves? I hated to think he fibbed. So I emailed his only surviving sibling at the time, Cornelia (Matson) Wing, and asked her about our relationship to Ralph Waldo Emerson. She wrote back with the same story Dad had told me, which she said originated with their grandmother, Katie Emerson (David). Katie told them she used to spend her summers at Ralph Waldo's home. But Katie was born in Kentucky and spent her youth in Illinois. She was never in Massachusetts, home of Ralph Waldo nor New York, home of Ralph Waldo's brother.

I was relieved. My father had not fibbed. My maternal great grandmother had. This also helped me to understand how a family can become confused as to who their ancestors were. Now I realize family tree research is a must. Verification is a must.

Dad had told the truth as he knew it, except maybe on where I got my name. On the latter point, I guess he didn't realize a four-year-old's memory can last a lifetime.

I told my siblings. My brother had named his son Emerson after Ralph Waldo Emerson. Luckily, Dad's first name was Emerson, so he had a fallback position.

My family now accepts we are not related to anyone famous. We have found happiness with who we are.

Chapter Eleven
A Lakota Name

I BOUGHT A STATE-OF-THE-ART computer and editing software with the VA money. I could now edit my documentary with a more professional touch.

Once I got to editing, I began to realize I still had more questions. So I contacted the brothers, and they agreed to additional interviews. During these interviews, I asked questions the historians in the Little Bighorn chat room could not answer.

One question came from my readings prior to meeting the family. I wanted to know how the Native name "Roman Nose" came to be. When I first read it, I wondered why would a warrior carry a name referencing Rome, Italy. I was sure that most Natives living in the plains during the 1800s did not know Italy even existed. Yet none of the books questioned how this name came to be. Doug cleared the air for me. He said the name was misinterpreted and should have been "Roaming Nose" which signified a person who wanders through the village visiting different tipis.

Another question was why Crazy Horse named his baby daughter "They Are Afraid Of Her." After all, who's afraid of a baby? They told me they named her after Crazy Horse's aunt. He wanted his daughter to have the same independent qualities as his aunt. They also told me their grandmother was named Iron Cedar because she was born near petrified wood.

They gave me so much information, I realized I needed to make more than a single documentary to cover it all. We decided to make three more feature-length documentaries, for a total of four. Each documentary after the first one would pertain to a time period within their oral history.

When we finished the first installment, we called it *The Authorized Biography of Crazy Horse and His Family, Part One.* We now had a way for their family's oral history to be known to the world.

With our documentary in hand, I expected the world would be as hungry for their family's information as I had been. I pitched it to cable TV companies, film distributors, and independent movie theaters. I even drove out to Hollywood with Floyd, Doug, and Don to add authenticity to my pitch. However, to my dismay, they told me they didn't accept programs from independent filmmakers, and the few who did said it lacked the "tried and true" story formula audiences craved. We did not feel the family's story lent itself to being restricted to cookie-cutter formulas. The family wanted the freedom to tell their truth.

I recommended we make our documentaries into DVDs and sell them at stores specializing in Native products—businesses that would be friendlier to our efforts. They agreed. These efforts met with mediocre success.

Don, Floyd, William, and Doug in Los Angeles

Thus, I created a website offering our DVDs directly to the public. As a result, even though our sales were less than robust, we developed an audience.

There is nothing easy about distributing stories about Natives in the United States, especially if you wanted to keep true to their original stories. Nearly 40 percent of our DVD sales came from Europe. The Europeans were more receptive to the truth about Crazy Horse and the Natives. Maybe it was because the Europeans felt less guilt over the Native's plight, because it did not happen on their soil—even though the early Americans were mostly children of Europe. Americans seemed to be content to ignore Native stories so they would not be reminded that their nation took Native lands by force, bullying, starvation, and bloodshed.

I sent a copy of our Crazy Horse DVD to Ernie. After he viewed it, he asked if he and I could make another attempt at a documentary on his oral history. I agreed. That summer I visited Ernie frequently to record the interviews we needed for the documentary. This time he made himself readily available. However, during our interviews, I got the feeling Ernie was still a little leery of giving me his full trust. He said he trusted me, but there didn't seem to be much in those initial interviews that wasn't already common knowledge. In my heart, I knew he had more to tell.

I took another tack. I remembered the day he had told Billeck in the heat of the moment that One Bull had helped murder Sitting Bull. So I asked him how he knew that. He hesitated and then replied he wasn't ready to divulge that information.

For the next few weeks, I did everything I could to make him feel comfortable enough to tell me personal stories. One night while we were eating supper, he described the method his mother used whenever she wanted him to stay in the house and hear one of their family stories about Sitting Bull. Ernie wasn't always interested in hearing her stories. He often wanted to play outside instead.

As a youngster, he and his parents lived in a small house on the Pine Ridge Rez. They had no electricity and carried their water into the house from a well. His mother used a kerosene lamp to illuminate their home at night.

One evening, to get him to stay and listen to his family's stories, she gathered him along with his niece Gloria and nephew Willard, who were around the same age, and told them when the sun went down the "See-oko" and "See-haha," beings, who liked to eat little boys and girls, would come out. Expecting Ernie would be skeptical, she enlisted the help of Ernie's older brother and his cousin to dress in rags and exit their root cellar after dark. Ernie told me when he saw them run out in their rags and duck behind the barn, he got frightened. It convinced him to stay indoors and listen to his family's oral history.

After he finished, I asked, "Why didn't you tell me that story during our interview? That's the kind of story that people are hungry to hear."

Ernie smiled. From that point on, he became more comfortable telling the stories his mother had told him in front of my camera. The "See-oko" and "See-haha" story is the opening scene for the second of our two-part series on his great grandfather's oral history.

Later on, he told me how he knew One Bull helped kill Sitting Bull. To paraphrase it, he said his mother told him that back when she was a youngster while riding in the back of a buckboard with her mother, Standing Holy, sitting up front, a Native man on horseback approached. The man greeted Standing Holy, who immediately covered her face and refused to look at him.

When the man begged her not to be so dismissive, she continued to refuse to look at him. Finally, he gave up and rode away. After he left, Ernie's mother asked her mom why she had acted like that when the man seemed so nice. That's when her mother identified the man as One Bull and said he was a spy for Standing Rock's federal agent, James McLaughlin. McLaughlin hated Sitting Bull. She told her daughter One Bull had ridden all night to carry a message to him saying Sitting Bull, who McLaughlin ordered to never leave the rez without his permission, was leaving anyway to meet with the Lakota agency head man, Red Cloud, on the Red Cloud Agency (rez). He wanted to discuss what to do about the ghost dance that was scaring white people. Upon receiving One Bull's message, McLaughlin sent his Indian police to stop Sitting Bull.

Once they arrived, they arrested him. While removing him from his cabin a scuffle broke out. During the scuffle, the police shot him in the chest and head, killing him. Sitting Bull was unarmed.

Preserving his oral history on video meant the world would know the family truth about Sitting Bull. Ernie was one of only two healthy surviving children at the time who heard his mother's stories first hand. The other was his nearly deaf older sister, Marlene. Gloria and Willard had both passed away, and his eldest sister Lydia was in a nursing home suffering from dementia.

Sadly, Lydia died in September 2009. Marlene passed away in March 2011. Ernie is now the last survivor at this writing.

Knowing his family's oral history needed more than a video, I asked him if I could help put his oral history in writing. He declined my offer, but thankfully he wrote a book on his own called *Sitting Bull: His Life and Legacy*. It packs more detail than I have written here, and it is directly from Ernie.

That winter I edited the footage we shot. We agreed to name it *The Authorized Biography of Sitting Bull by His Great Grandson, Part One*. It would be the first of a two-part DVD series.

Once we finished Part One, we promoted it the same way as the Crazy Horse documentary. Many of those who bought the Crazy Horse video bought the one for Sitting Bull. Ernie and Sonja brought new buyers into the mix, too. While promoting the DVD, people occasionally asked Ernie about Crazy Horse and other Native warriors. Ernie always replied that he could only talk about his own family's oral history. Questions about other warriors' oral histories needed to be directed to the families of those warriors. To interpret another family's oral history without permission would make him no different than the historians he complained about.

With Ernie's first DVD in the can, I switched gears and concentrated on Part Two of the Crazy Horse documentary series. I visited several more Crazy Horse sites with Floyd, Doug, and Don. I interviewed the local spokesperson at these sites and juxtaposed what they said against what Floyd, Doug, and Don said. When the stories were compared side by side, the family's stories always made more sense and thus more honest.

At the same time, I worked with Ernie to collect additional footage to finish his two-part series.

Once on a trip to the Lakota and Cheyenne's sacred site of Deer Medicine Rock, with Ernie and tour guide Serle Chapman, we visited with Jack Bailey. During my visit, I found myself alone with Serle in Jack's kitchen. I causally mentioned the Clown family's Owl Rock story, and Serle replied he didn't think Floyd, Doug, and Don were related to Crazy Horse. Jack, who heard us from another room, entered the kitchen and said in a rising voice, "I believe that they are the family! Do you want to know why?"

He did not wait for a reply.

"Because when they came, it was their first time, but they already knew about everything that was here. That's why! You know, I've shown those carvings to a great many people in my life, but I encountered no first-time visitors who knew exactly what was here unless they came for Sitting Bull's vision, which everybody knows about from books. They knew about the Crazy Horse carving and how

Deer Medicine Rocks
Photo by Mark Frethem

to read it before I knew how to read it." Then Jack stopped and shook his head in disbelief, "Those guys just know things that nobody else knows."

Jack, who was in his late seventies, struck me as a humble man who rarely got riled up. Jack had seen, heard, and experienced more regarding those carvings, than anyone else alive. His family had owned the land where the sacred rocks stood since the 1880s. His grandmother was a favorite interpreter of the Northern Cheyenne, because as a little girl she had picked up their language while playing with the Cheyenne children. Being so young, the Cheyenne knew they could trust her because her youth made her incapable of lying.

Jack came to his conclusion on the Clowns differently than I had. His was through a lifetime of experiences with both Native and non-Native "experts" surmising what the carvings meant, and then hearing the Clowns. Jack was spiritual, and his spiritual senses along with his past experiences with other Natives that had seen the rock told him that what the Clowns were saying was true. Unfortunately, Jack passed away October 7, 2019, at age eighty-eight.

A few months later, Floyd, Doug, and Don informed me Kevin had taken a job at a US Army Recruiting Station. That meant he could not accompany us on any trips to the sites we needed to visit. He was not an active participant on any of our trips, almost from the time I had known him, so it did not come as a surprise. When winter came, I again brought Floyd, Doug, and Don to Portland so I could record them at Mark's studio.

Those who really loved Crazy Horse and had watched our Part One DVD shared it with others. Even though our sales were anemic, the enthusiasm they engendered made several authors and scholars nervous—authors and scholars that depended on their own versions of Crazy Horse's life story for their income. Despite our exposure being minimal, they felt compelled to spend the energy to discredit the family and myself, confirming they considered the family's stories a threat to their own credibility. It told us if we could somehow get the family's entire oral history into the hands of a larger audience, it could change how people understood the life of Crazy Horse and his family.

During a break at Mark's studio, Doug surprised and honored me by giving me a Lakota name: "Cante Iste Ewonke," which he said meant "He Sees Through the Eye of His Heart." My heart melted in gratitude. I could feel my father looking down from above, with a smile.

Years later Floyd told me that to be accurate, Lakota language-wise, and convey the meaning Doug intended, my name should read "Cante Iste Ogna Ewonke." He also said Doug did not have permission to give me the name. However, I had already accepted it. Maybe I'll get a new name sometime in the future. If not, I'm more than happy with the one I have.

Once we wrapped up the interviews, they went back to the rez.

About two months later, Floyd, Doug, and Don called to say their Crazy Horse Estate court case was having a hearing at the Rosebud Rez's Tribal Courthouse. So I drove to the rez, picked them up, and drove them to the hearing.

Both the other family claimants, Seth Big Crow and Harvey White Woman, had passed away. Frederick Little Bald Eagle was appointed to take Big Crow's place representing the Rosebud Rez, while Doug Bissonette was appointed to the replace White Woman from the Pine Ridge Rez.

The premise for the hearing was to interview Lakota elders to learn how the heirs for the Crazy Horse Estate would have been designated at the time of his death in 1877 and how that might translate in today's world.

To determine this, three elder mediators were chosen. Karen Lone Hill represented Pine Ridge Rez, Marilyn Circle Eagle represented Cheyenne River Rez, and they chose Webster Two Hawk as the third representative.

After all the claimants gathered at the Rosebud Tribal Courthouse, the Rosebud Tribal Judge Sherman Marshall ruled the court would postpone the interviews because one elder could not attend due to a family emergency. After adjourning, he invited the claimants to hold their own meeting in his courtroom.

He then retired to his chambers, but kept his door open to watch what took place.

The Clown's attorney, Cheryl Bogue, was not there that day. The attorney representing Rosebud and Pine Ridge's claimants, Bob Gough, asked everyone to hear his proposal. We did.

He said Floyd, Doug, and Don should come together as one with his Rosebud and Pine Ridge clients to share the ownership of the Crazy Horse Estate. When he asked if they would accept his proposal, the Clown family declined. With that, our time in the courtroom came to a close.

A few weeks later I heard that the court interviews with the elders were completed over the phone. They found in 1877, Crazy Horse's father Waglula would have inherited Crazy Horse's belongings, name, and spiritual possessions. Thus, only those who descended from Old Man Crazy Horse could inherit the Crazy Horse Estate. The Clown family claimed victory. But after the ruling, the Rosebud and Pine Ridge representatives and their legal council adopted a strategy of delaying the final ruling.

Over the next two years, I completed Ernie's second-part DVD and finished the first three installments of our four-part series on Crazy Horse. During this time the Crazy Horse family informed me that Kevin had been called back to active military service and would deploy to Afghanistan. They understood writing a book while trying to stay alive in a combat zone would be too hard.

The book they wanted him to write would now be without a writer. Floyd, Doug, and Don considered the book the most important piece in getting their oral history out to the public, over and above the documentaries we had made.

With the need for a new author, I offered my services. However, they said they were considering someone else who had already written and published a book, who lived on the east coast.

After working on and then trying to distribute the DVDs, I had come to the same conclusion as the family that a book, as my father had originally suggested, was the most effective way to get their truth of the story out in the world. However, my chances of being chosen didn't seem good. My not having ever written a book was a liability.

I was discouraged. I needed a change.

So, I surprised everybody, including myself, and moved to San Jose, California. Not that I had a particular fondness for San Jose, but I had met a girl who lived there. She told me the city was an oasis of creativity. I believed her.

Chapter Twelve
The Book

IN RETROSPECT, MOVING TO San Jose was good. I had the peace and quiet to create. However, the woman I moved there for and I parted ways. We never really connected.

I still harbored hopes of writing the family's book. While perusing the internet, I found a bargain airline flight from Rapid City to Las Vegas, one way. I could drive them home. Being in Las Vegas together would allow me to make one last plea to write their book. When I suggested the trip, they agreed.

We spent three days there. I brought up my availability to write their book several times. Each time it was met with silence. When our time in Las Vegas came to an end, I felt I had failed in my mission to convince them to be their writer.

During our drive back to the rez, they discussed who might replace Kevin. My entire body screamed "pick me," but I stayed quiet. I had stated my case. Now, I figured if they wanted me, they would say so. Finally, Floyd asked if I would write their book. His words were heaven sent.

A lively discussion followed. We agreed I would write it after I wrapped up the final installment of our Crazy Horse DVD series.

I knew at least one chapter would be devoted to the family's stories about the Little Bighorn battle. It would be as my father wished—a story of the battle from the Native side.

Upon returning home, I edited the fourth part in record time, at least compared to my previous efforts. After they approved it for release, I was ready to write.

Because Floyd, Doug, and Don were telling me their family's personal history, we agreed they would have last say on every word that went in the book.

The first chapter was taken from things I had heard from them and other family members during the decade I had known them. It was meant to set the tone for the rest of the book.

William, Doug, and Delmar Clown (Floyd's older brother) listen to Doug as he explains how the Deer Medicine Rocks Sundance of 1876 was laid out. Photo by Mark Frethem.

After that I listened to their stories, writing them down the way I heard them, in the first person. I did not want to put myself between them and the readers. Once I finished the manuscript in late 2010, I handed it to them for review and corrections.

Their corrections were many. I addressed them with my revisions. Then they would ask me to revise my revisions. There were times I felt like I would never make them happy. Sometimes I longed to be like Niehardt, author of *Black Elk Speaks*, and print what I wrote and not worry about having my work corrected. After six months of rewrites, our efforts finally came together.

Then something happened that would upset our apple cart for a long time. Floyd got arrested for having marijuana.

While he was awaiting sentencing, we worked to finish the final corrections on the book. On June 2, 2011, they sentenced Floyd to twenty-eight months in prison. I did not see or talk to him for two years. I find it ironic that they sentenced him to so much jail time for something that today is legal in many states, even in South Dakota, the state he was arrested in. But it is not uncommon for Natives to get harsher sentences than normal.

During his incarceration, I looked to the next eldest brother, Doug, for leadership. Doug took his role seriously. He said the family wanted the definitions of our compensation spelled out in a legal contract before we went to a publisher.

For a book, we would need an entertainment lawyer. However, most were not licensed to practice law in South Dakota. Finally, I found one in Minneapolis. After drawing up our contract, our job became how to get the book published.

It was around this time I received phone calls from Ernie asking to do another documentary. He said a documentary filmmaker from the National Geographic Channel had approached him. Ernie said he didn't trust him. Ernie wanted this film to be about his repatriation with Sitting Bull's lock of hair and to set in motion moving his great grandfather's bones to a place only his family would know.

During my time working on part two of *Sitting Bull's Authorized Biography by His Great Grandson*, Billeck called Ernie to say he had concluded his investigation and was ready to repatriate the hair and leggins to Ernie and his sisters. He invited Ernie and Sonja to the Smithsonian in Washington, DC, for a repatriation ceremony. Ernie then invited me and my camera to come with them. Around the first of December Ernie, Sonja, and I drove to Washington, DC.

During our drive, Ernie told me a DNA expert from the University of Copenhagen, Eske Willerslev, had contacted him. He had read about repatriation efforts in the *New York Times* and had called to inquire about getting Sitting Bull's hair and extracting the DNA, to help prove or disprove anyone's claim of being related to Sitting Bull. Ernie told me he could not tell Willerslev yes or no because the hair did not belong to him. It belonged to Sitting Bill. Sitting Bull would have to give permission. That would require a ceremony.

We made it to Washington the day before the ceremony. On December 5, 2007, the Smithsonian held a special repatriation presentation that declared Ernie and his sisters the closest living relatives to Sitting Bull. They gave Ernie the hair and leggins. I was privileged and honored to video the proceedings.

Once we returned to South Dakota, Ernie proposed a ceremony to ask Sitting Bull's spirit if the hair and leggins belonged to him. He asked his friend Marvin Helper, a medicine man, to conduct the ceremony in his home. Ernie also invited Willerslev, so he could find out if Sitting Bull deemed him worthy of having the lock of his hair once it was decided that it really was his hair. Willerslev accepted the invitation and flew in from Copenhagen. Billeck attended as a guest. Ernie's sisters Ethel and Marlene were also there. Lydia had passed away by that time.

Once we all sat on Ernie's basement floor, they turned the lights out. We could see nothing. Not even our hands directly in front of our faces. I sat on the west side of the room with my back against the wall. Directly across from me was Willerslev, with his back against the east wall. Once the ceremony began, the prayers were said in Lakota. They sang Lakota songs. Helper called for Sitting Bull's spirit. I found it hard to know exactly what was going on between the darkness and hearing a language I did not know whispered at the far end of the room.

Suddenly I heard a rattle shaking. The rattle landed gently on my head and stayed there for about three seconds. I did not understand why it landed on me and still don't to this day. About ten minutes later, the ceremony ended. The lights came on.

I was most eager to see what Sitting Bull had decided as far as ownership of his hair and leggins. So I approached Ernie and asked what Sitting Bull had said. Ernie explained that Sitting Bull said both the hair and leggins were his. Then I asked if he would permit Eske to take the hair to Copenhagen.

"My great grandfather told me he could take some but not all," Ernie replied.

"How much is some?" I queried.

"Less than half," Ernie answered, and with that he excused himself so he could discuss what Sitting Bull had said with his sisters.

Later I learned they would allow Eske three inches of the approximately foot long lock of hair.

Willerslev told me during a video interview that during the ceremony he saw a blue-green light approach him, crawl up his arm and disappear into his throat. He could not explain how this could be. He kept his legs fully extended and moving in front of him so he would feel anything or anybody that might be controlling the light. He could only feel empty space. Eske admitted he had no scientific explanation at all. Ernie informed him the blue-green light was Sitting Bull's spirit.

After using Ernie's repatriation ceremony footage in the *Authorized Biography of Sitting Bull by His Great*

Eske Willerslev

Grandson, Part Two, Ernie now wanted me to use the same footage on a documentary about his and Sitting Bull's DNA matching.

At the time the media industry was converting to a high-definition format. I still had the older, standard-definition technology. I encouraged Ernie to see the advantages of working with the National Geographic Channel over me. After all, the exposure of being on the National Geographic Channel and its corresponding financial opportunities and their more current technology were beyond what I could offer. But Ernie would have none of it, and finally I agreed to make his documentary. I was honored he thought that much of me, but I did not know how I would make it attractive to cable TV or consumers without access to an HD camera. So I contacted our mutual friend, Tim Prokop, to see if he could help.

Tim was a producer of a cable TV show that had included Ernie in a program called "History Hogs." I talked with him a few times on the phone at Ernie's suggestion, in hopes he could get my documentaries on TV—but nothing developed. However, we had kept our lines of communication open.

Ernie and Sonja asked me to live with them while we worked on his documentary. However, I was leery of moving in. The last time I stayed with them, they asked me to leave when things weren't moving quickly enough. Now I was armed only with the slim hope of getting the proper camera. As a result, I felt even less safe than the first time. However, when we talked, Sonja reassured me I wouldn't be kicked out again.

Trusting things could work out, I moved into their spare bedroom.

Once I moved in, Ernie and I had several meaningful conversations. He told me he had spent a few years living under a bridge in Denver as a homeless alcoholic, prior to his marriage to Sonja. It surprised me that the great grandson of one of the greatest leaders the world had known spent part of his life living under a bridge. I thought it would be an excellent story to tell about how he had worked his way from living on the streets to being a respected representative of Sitting Bull.

I suggested this story to both Ernie and Tim. They agreed it would be a good approach.

Knowing my camera situation, Tim offered to supply an HD camera, and in return he would be executive producer on the documentary. I brought his proposal to Ernie. Ernie was less than enthusiastic about teaming up with him. He said he didn't trust Tim. A few days later, Tim told me he would handle our distribution and get Ernie's documentary on TV.

Getting TV distribution and a camera broke the ice with Ernie. Finally, we all agreed to become equal partners. Now it was on to raise the money for travel and filming expenses. Tim went to bat first and tried to find someone to finance our film. He solicited several providers of cable TV content, but had no luck.

Then by chance I came across something on the internet called crowdfunding, a relatively new concept in 2012. In crowdfunding we could solicit donations for our project and in return reward the donors with a gift. There was one site, Kickstarter, that seemed reputable. So we made a promotional video for our project, devised rewards, wrote a description of our documentary, and put it on Kickstarter, hoping to raise twenty thousand dollars. Kickstarter gave us a little over a month to raise the money. However, according to their rules, if we were a penny short of our goal they would return all the money committed back to the original donors. It was all or nothing. Once we embarked on our campaign, I didn't sleep much. Thankfully, we reached our goal on the very last day of our allotted time.

Once production began, our unity evaporated. Tim wanted the production to be more of a historical piece that would be acceptable to a cable TV content provider, and Ernie wanted to use it to prove he was the great grandson of Sitting Bull and worthy of that title.

However, one thing we all wanted was to show Ernie and Sitting Bull's DNA matched. So I and my camera were invited to accompany Ernie and Sonja to Willerslev's DNA facility in Copenhagen.

During my time there I filmed how they extracted DNA. I had to cover myself in a white, clean suit, cover my hair with a paper hairnet, wear a mask over my mouth and nose, and use a covering over my shoes to film in the pre-clean rooms. I was not allowed to film in the clean rooms where the DNA was extracted. After a few days, Willerslev called Ernie, Sonja, and me in for a meeting. He confirmed Ernie's DNA and the DNA from Sitting Bull's lock of hair were a match. It confirmed what Ernie already knew.

I tried to make both Tim and Ernie happy, but I didn't succeed. We finished the documentary. It even won awards, but we never got the cable TV or the national exposure we desired.

We ended up calling our documentary *Sitting Bull's Voice.*

In the spring of 2013, I got a call from a familiar voice—Floyd. He had been released from prison a few months early and was now living at a halfway house. I caught him up on all that had taken place on our book since he had been away, which was nothing. He told me as soon as we could, we should reignite our search for a publisher.

Once he was released from the halfway house and out on parole, he took a job in construction with his friend, Mack Longbrake. Floyd and I would occasionally talk by phone. During one call, I shared what I had learned about Ernie's book publisher, Gibbs Smith. Ernie had encouraged me to contact them. Floyd liked the idea and suggested we go to Utah and present our book to them in person. I agreed.

However, my mother died on June 22, 2013, and suddenly my pursuit to find a publisher got put on hold.

Chapter Thirteen
A Gift

BY MAY 2015, MY mom's affairs were finally in order. I moved to Spearfish, South Dakota, to be nearer to the Clowns and Ernie. Floyd helped me move.

In July, Floyd and I finally made our trip to Layton, Utah, to see Ernie's publisher, Gibbs Smith. They asked us to leave the manuscript and said they would get back to us. So we did. We figured it would be several months before they gave us an answer. However, much to our surprise, it wasn't.

The owner, Gibbs Smith, for whom the company was named, had presented our story to a German publisher who asked to publish a German translation of it. With that commitment in hand, they said they would publish it in English on the condition that we would promote it in the US on our own. They scheduled the release date for spring 2016. I called Ernie to thank him for recommending his publisher. Ernie said he was happy for us and sent his congratulations.

In August, I got a phone call from Doug Bissonette one of the claimants in the court battle for heirship of the Crazy Horse estate. He said Ernie gave him my number. Bissonette called to warn me that if I allowed our book to go to press it would be considered fiction, because he and his relatives were the only true heirs of Crazy Horse.

"You should do the book with me," he suggested.

I told him I was satisfied the Clown family was the genuine family and asked him to not contact me unless he could present a legal family tree complete with probates, allotments, census, enrollment, ration, and church records to back it up. He did not address my request for any of those documents, instead he got angry.

I then called Ernie to ask why he gave my number to Bissonette. He told me he thought Bissonette's story would interest me. I told him until Bissonette could present a legal tree proving his ties, there was no reason for me to talk to him. At that point, I thought the entire episode was water under the bridge.

Later that same day, Bissonette sent about a dozen unsolicited emails, each containing a historical document he felt supported his claim—none of them being the documents I had asked for. After reviewing his documents, I found they had originated almost entirely from non-Native sources—sources I had previously found and researched. I had questioned the Clowns on their relevance years before. They said they weren't accurate. The people that wrote them were the same people who had taken their Lakota way of living life away from them. It was their version of history. History nearly always is written to reflect well on those still in power.

Bissonette also sent a tentative family tree that had not been backed by the supporting documents I had asked for. Interestingly enough, its author was the historian, Dickson, from the chat room, who had not kept his promise to meet with Doug.

Having not been presented with any compelling arguments for halting our manuscript from being published, I made the decision to ignore any future Bissonette emails that lacked the evidence I sought.

Then something sinister happened. Gibbs Smith informed me and the family on September 11 that they were putting a hold on publishing our book because a lawyer representing the families contesting the Clown's claim to the estate had contacted them. He questioned the legality of our having our book printed, even though Floyd was appointed by the court to be one of the administrators of the Crazy Horse estate.

It stunned me. I didn't think they had any legal grounds to stop publication. However, Gibbs Smith wanted their legal department to take a look, anyway.

The lawyer who had contacted them was the same one who represented the Rosebud and Pine Ridge administrators in court, Bob Gough. Simultaneously, Bissonette was inundating Gibbs Smith with the same emails he had previously sent to me. It was an attempt to get them to remove our book from their publication schedule permanently.

It is one thing to argue against what we had put in our book. It was another to keep it from the light of day.

I vowed to do everything in my power to make sure our book got published. It got my adrenaline flowing. To fight this unwarranted censorship, I called our publisher to reason and plead for them not to deny us publication. As a result, they asked to speak to the Clown's legal representative, Cheryl Bogue. Once they talked to her, the publishing house's legal team huddled to decide.

We waited with baited breath for several days.

Finally, they made their decision. After having done their due diligence, they decided in our favor. They would publish our book in its entirety and unedited. The new release date was fall 2016. We breathed a sigh of relief.

We got to work building a Facebook page in preparation of fulfilling our promise to publicize our book. The family named our page "Tashunke Witko Tiwahe," which in the Lakota language means "Crazy Horse Family." We added the English translation of "Crazy Horse Family" to follow their chosen name since most people didn't understand the Lakota language. It still exists as of this writing.

Not long afterwards, I hosted Arne Martin Boe on a visit to the US from Norway. Arne had contributed some money to help *Sitting Bull's Voice* get made through our crowdfunding a few years earlier. After making his donation, he made a trip across the Atlantic to meet with Ernie and me in 2012. Arne and I hit it off and became fast friends. I happened to say during his visit I had a Norwegian great grandmother but did not know her maiden name. When he returned home, he spent hours and hours helping to find my Norwegian roots. It was an extraordinary act of selflessness. Once he had done it, it was impossible for me to thank him enough. Nearly all of what I know about my Norwegian roots I owe to him.

I also asked him about the possibility of doing a translation of our book into Norwegian. He wholeheartedly agreed. After participating in a sweat lodge ceremony with

Arne Martin Boe

the family, he got their permission. Then he flew home to wait for a published version so he could translate it into Norwegian.

Gibbs Smith released our English language book September 6, 2016. Our first book signing was in Rapid City, at Books-A-Million. Previous to our event, I envisioned crowds of people would wait to meet us and buy a copy. My hopes were crushed when only about fifteen people showed up.

The second signing at the Prairie Pages Bookstore in Pierre, South Dakota, was much better. A steady stream of people buying and wanting us to sign their books met us. We followed that signing with another one at the South Dakota Historical Society, where we were also well received. Speaking to a packed and attentive audience for the first time about something that had taken so much passion, work, and perseverance to get published was where we felt the full gravity of what we had accomplished. We were all emotional. Sometimes we had to stop our presentation and collect ourselves before we could continue.

Our experiences encouraged us to present ourselves elsewhere. I contacted bookstores in Wyoming, Nebraska, and South Dakota. Once they agreed to host us, we set out on our first road trip. Our first stop was in Cheyenne, Wyoming. When we arrived, the bookstore manager had forgotten he had agreed to host us. He greeted us by asking if we had brought our own table and chairs for signing the books. We thought he was joking, but once we realized he was serious, we scrambled to put together a makeshift signing table from an abandoned rolling book cart and ended up sitting on plastic magazine storage boxes while we signed. It was a humbling experience.

After Cheyenne, the bulk of our road trip was in Nebraska. Those that attended our talks appreciated our information.

In between tour dates, I took time to see a woman I had met from the Philippines. Her name was Mae. We

Doug, Floyd, and William prepare for a book talk

Mae and her daughters Alisa and Andrea

fell in love. Mae agreed to be my wife. We married October 1, 2017.

In early 2018, while touring the western half of the United States, Arne got our Norwegian translation published. To promote it, he put together a crowdfunding effort in Norway to bring us to Scandinavia for book signings. After his crowdfunding succeeded, he got us airline tickets for early summer 2018.

Once Floyd, Doug, and I landed in Copenhagen, Arne picked us up in an RV. Our first stop was on June 3, at the Gjethest Museum in Frederiksvaerk, Denmark, thirty-four miles north of Copenhagen. We drew around one hundred people.

The next morning, we had breakfast in Copenhagen with two of the donors from Arne's crowdfunding efforts, Kaj Clausen and Peder Skytte. Skytte is a singer and songwriter. He sang a song for us that included a reference

*Floyd, William, and Doug enter the Arctic Circle
on their way to Alta, Norway*

to Crazy Horse. It was moving. Arne ended up putting together a documentary of our trip and Skytte's song is in it. The documentary is available on the internet at: vimeo.com/ondemand/crazyhorseiskandinavia

After Denmark, we drove north through Sweden and Finland to one of the most northern outposts in Scandinavia, a place called Alta, Norway. Over the next seventeen days, we had stops in the Norwegian cities of Storsteinnes, Svolver, Trondheim, Bergen, Burne, Tvedestrand, and Kolbotn. They were all well attended.

After our last stop, Arne left us. Now on our own, we caught a bus to Kumla, Sweden, to visit another friend, Curt Wahrme.

While in Sweden, Curt took us to the Etnografiska Museum in Stockholm for a book talk. A sizable crowd greeted us. It was at this talk that I met many of my Swedish relatives for the first time. I had met my cousin, Ingrid

Doug, Curt Wahrme, and Floyd at Curt's place in Sweden

Tunhammar, on a previous trip to Sweden, which Curt had set up. Just as with Arne, it is impossible to thank Curt enough. When I saw Ingrid in the audience with her family—my family—I got choked up. I could feel their support, even though I had met none of them other than the briefest of introductions prior to the talk. It was the best feeling in the world. I got together with them after the talk—something I will forever cherish. We stayed at Ingrid's house for a few days and then took a plane to London, where we had our last book signing.

After a brief break upon our return from Europe, we continued our touring. It was now just Floyd and me. Mae became our book seller. Occasionally Floyd had his son, Floyd Jr., or his grandson, Phoenix, travel with us, but they never spoke at our signings unless they were answering an occasional question from the audience.

During our tour Floyd and I drove to all our destinations. During one of those drives I asked him for an explanation of what happened to the Flathead band of the Lakota.

"They went north," Floyd answered.

"Where in the north?" I asked.

"I don't know," Floyd replied.

I had wanted to hear something more. However, Floyd has always told the truth on serious matters. So, out of respect, I made the conscious decision to continue to seek third-party documents or testimonials that backed up his contention. Once I document them, I will write another book.

One of our first talks after our return from Europe was at the Crazy Horse School in Wamblee, on the Pine Ridge Reservation.

The school called an assembly for us to speak to the entire student body. After our talk, they honored us by presenting both Floyd and me with star quilt blankets. Then the entire student body sang an honoring song with each student and faculty member shaking our hands. We were quite moved.

On February 29, 2020, we gave our last scheduled talk. Our talks total 317, at this writing.

Now the Clown family's goal is to get the Crazy Horse Agency—their sacred Black Hills—back. It is their people's burial grounds. During our talks Floyd encouraged people to think of the Black Hills in the same way they thought of a cemetery built alongside a church. Only the Lakota cemetery had people living on it and driving all over it. When one sees the Black Hills as the place where their deceased relatives lay, it is easy to understand why the passion to get them back is so strong.

I have no regrets about having spent the last eighteen years working with the Crazy Horse family. No regrets

Floyd and William speak at the Seven Circles Heritage Center near Peoria, Il. Floyd and William were speakers at every one of the 317 talks.

about the time I spent with Ernie and Sonja and learning the Sitting Bull family oral history.

Even though Ernie and the Clowns did not know each other prior to my arrival, some of their age-old stories had similarities. For instance, the Clowns said that Custer's brother, Tom, was killed at the Little Bighorn River in the first moments of Custer's attack, sending the soldiers into a hasty retreat. Ernie said when he was a little boy, Dewey Beard would come to visit his uncles, John Sitting Bull and Little Soldier, at his home. They would talk about the battle. He said his mother told him that they agreed someone important was killed at the Little Bighorn River in the first moments of battle, sending the soldiers into an unorganized retreat. Although there were minor differences, the similarity in their stories was quite strong.

Prior to publishing our book, I met with Jim Jandreau at Bear Butte. He told me he had known that the Clown family was the Crazy Horse family as a youngster. He learned of it while attending St. Joseph's Indian School in Chamberlain, South Dakota, in the 1960s. In the schoolyard those who spoke Lakota would talk about the Clown family connection. If you didn't know Lakota, then you were likely to be left out of the loop. I will always be grateful to him for trusting me and putting me in touch with the family.

But to be honest, it is my father who deserves the most credit for directing me onto a path for both of us to walk together and help the truth get out.

Although this journey has not enriched me financially, it has given me as rewarding and as rich an experience as life can offer. An experience that no amount of money could buy.

Floyd has proposed to make me a brother in a Hunka ceremony. That would make me a part of the Crazy Horse family—something that we are both sure will confuse people when they met me, learn of it, and see that I am white.

When my father requested I finish what he had started, I thought I was fulfilling an obligation. Now I realize it was really a gift.

I know my father will be the first person to come get me when I am ready to go to the other side.

Emerson Nels Matson, 1926-1998

CPSIA information can be obtained
at www.ICGtesting.com
Printed in the USA
LVHW080219250922
729205LV00025B/550

9 781735 867007